INCREDIBLE
SCIENCE
EXPERIMENTS
TO AMAZE YOUR FRIENDS

ARCTURUS

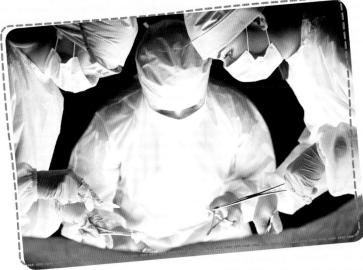

ARCTURUS

This edition published in 2017 by Arcturus Publishing Limited
26/27 Bickels Yard, 151–153 Bermondsey Street,
London SE1 3HA

Author: Thomas Canavan
Designer: Elaine Wilkinson
Editors: Frances Evans, Becca Clunes

Picture credits:
All images courtesy of Shutterstock, apart from:
Getty / Digital Light Source: p. 33 t.

ISBN 978-1-78428-465-7
CH005181US
Supplier: 26, Date 1216, Print run 5146

Printed in China

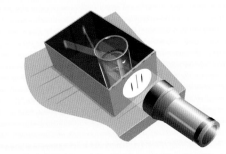

Contents

Having Fun and Being Safe

Inside this book you'll find a whole range of exciting science experiments that can be performed safely at home. Nearly all the equipment you need will be found around your own house. Anything that you don't have at home should be available at a local store.

We have given some recommendations alongside the instructions to let you know when adult help might be needed. However, the degree of adult supervision will vary, depending on the age of the child and the experiment. We would recommend close adult supervision for any experiment involving cooking equipment, sharp implements, electrical equipment, or batteries.

The author and publisher cannot take responsibility for any injury, damage, or mess that might occur as a result of attempting the experiments in this book. Always tell an adult before you perform any experiments, and follow the instructions carefully.

Forces

Whether you're lifting books with your breath or examining moonlike craters in a baking pan, you'll be able to demonstrate how scientific forces lie behind just about everything!

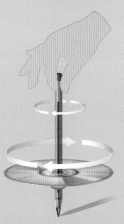

Launch your very own rocket (p. 24)!

Some Light Reading

YOU WILL NEED

- 3 hardbound books (about 200 pages each)
- Masking tape
- Plastic drinking straw
- A small plastic shopping bag
- Table

A pile of textbooks is pretty heavy to carry around, isn't it? But can you imagine being able to lift that same pile using just your breath? It seems easy enough to lift a sheet of paper or a feather with just your breath, but something as heavy as a stack of books? Is there a scientific trick waiting to be learned?

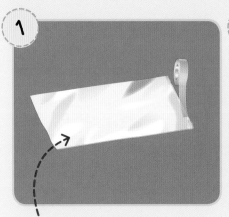

1 Tape the handle and open end of the bag shut, leaving just enough space to slide a straw inside it.

2 Place the bag close to the edge of the table, with the taped end facing you.

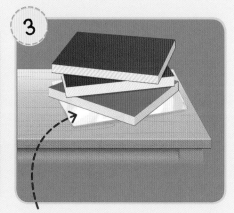

3 Pile the books on the bag.

4 Slide the straw into the gap in the bag and blow into it. The bag will begin to inflate and lift the books.

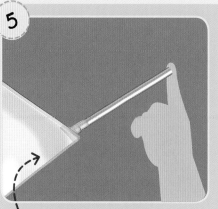

5 Stop to catch your breath, blocking the end of the straw to stop air from escaping.

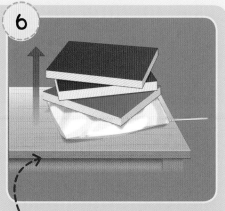

6 Continue inflating the bag until the books have risen 1–2 inches.

HOW DOES IT WORK?

You've just demonstrated Pascal's Law, first noted by French scientist Blaise Pascal in the seventeenth century. It deals with fluids, the term that scientists use to describe both liquids and gases. The law describes what happens if an outside force (in this case, your breath) is applied to an enclosed fluid (the air inside the bag). The force is transmitted equally throughout the fluid. You might think that your breath is a small force, but it is pressing equally all across the bag. That multiplied force then becomes strong enough to lift the books.

TOP TIP!

Make sure that the straw fits snugly inside the opening of the bag, with no gaps. You might even find it easier to slide the straw in first and then tape the end of the bag shut.

WHAT HAPPENS IF...?

Maybe you've done a variation of this experiment—in reverse. If you poke a blown-up balloon, you'll see it bulge out in all directions. That's because the force of your finger's pressure has been spread equally through the air inside the balloon. With enough force, it will burst.

REAL-LIFE SCIENCE

Have you ever seen a car lifted high up, so that a mechanic can work on its underside? It rises on a hydraulic jack. The jack that lifted the car worked on the same principle as your inflating bag—except that it was liquid (not air) receiving the extra force.

Last Man Standing

Someone who's easy to beat in a game is called a pushover. Here's a chance to use some science to decide which of three similar cartons is the real pushover. You might be surprised at the result!

YOU WILL NEED

- 3 empty fruit juice cartons (59 fl oz) with screw-on caps
- Water
- Marker pen
- Table
- Measuring stick or long ruler
- Note pad

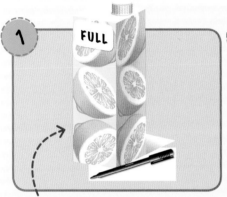

1 Fill one carton with water, screw the cap back on and mark it "Full."

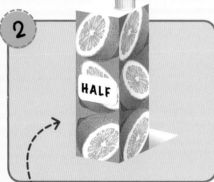

2 Half-fill a second, replace the cap, and mark it "Half."

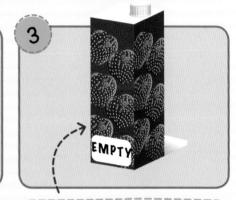

3 Screw the cap back on to the third carton and mark it "Empty."

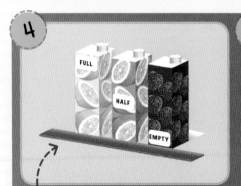

4 Use the measuring stick to line all three straight alongside each other on the table. Stop to consider and predict which of the three cartons is most stable.

5 Line the measuring stick behind the three cartons, touching them lightly about 2 inches down from the top.

6 Push the stick forward very slowly and observe which of the cartons is the first, second, and third to fall.

HOW DOES IT WORK?

This experiment is all about center of mass—the point in any object that represents the average location of its mass. You can imagine all of the object's mass being concentrated at that point. In practical terms, the center of mass determines how stable an object is. If it remains above the object's base of support (like the base of the cartons), then the object remains stable. The center of mass of the full—and empty—cartons was about halfway up the carton. But the half-full carton's center of mass was in the lower half because the top half (air) had less mass.

TOP TIP!

Make sure that you have the measuring stick actually touching all three cartons before you move them.

WHAT HAPPENS IF...?

You could do this experiment over and over, filling the cartons to different levels, to find the amount of water that leads to the most stable result. Your first version showed that the carton with some water worked best. Would a one-third full carton be more secure? What about one that's one-quarter full?

REAL-LIFE SCIENCE

The center of mass is important in all kinds of areas—from industry to entertainment. Just think of a group of acrobats forming a pyramid. If you drew an imaginary line down from the top acrobat's center of mass, it would end up safely in the middle of the person at the bottom (the base).

Up to the Water Mark

We know that firefighters use hoses that work under enormous pressure to send the water great distances—high up into tall buildings, for example. But you don't need special equipment to understand how water behaves when it's under pressure.

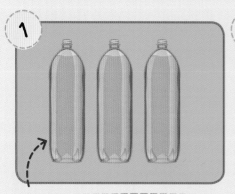

1 Fill each bottle completely with tap water.

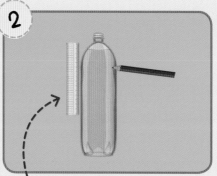

2 Ask an adult to use the pencil to poke a hole as wide as the pencil in the first bottle—about 2 inches down from the top. Ask a friend to plug the hole with their finger.

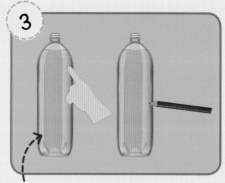

3 Repeat step 2 for the second bottle, but with the hole about midway down.

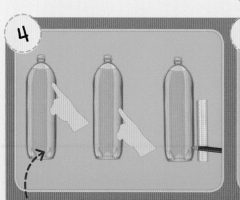

4 Do the same for the third bottle, poking the hole 1–2 inches from the bottom. Each friend should now be plugging a bottle.

5 Line the bottles up, 2 feet apart, with the holes pointing in the same direction. Get your friends to pull their fingers away, one by one, and note how far each stream of water shoots.

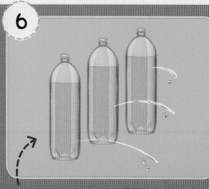

6 Measure the longest point of each stream of water.

HOW DOES IT WORK?

It was a force that sent the water flying out of those three holes. And one of the great observations of Sir Isaac Newton was that a force is a combination of something's mass and its acceleration. In each case, the water was falling (because of gravity) with the same acceleration. The big difference was mass, or how much mass was bearing down on the water by the hole. The bottom hole had nearly a full bottle of water weighing down on it: all that extra mass meant more force; enough to shoot the water the farthest.

TOP TIP!

Things can get a little messy, so make sure you do this experiment outside!

WHAT HAPPENS IF...?

You've worked out how the extra mass of water creates a stronger pressure, forcing the water out farther as the pressure increases. What if you did the experiment with larger, or smaller, holes in the bottles? Would the difference in "shooting length" remain the same?

REAL-LIFE SCIENCE

You've probably experienced the relationship between water pressure and depth when you've been swimming. The deeper you swim, the more pressure you feel, especially on your ears (which are sensitive to pressure). It's the same principle that explains the science behind this experiment.

The Attractive Balloon

YOU WILL NEED

- A strong balloon (round is better than long)
- At least six light plastic cups (6 fl oz)
- Some water

Of course you want guests to stick around at your birthday party. But plastic cups? Stuck to a party balloon? That's not the right idea. But wait—how did those cups end up stuck to the balloon in the first place? A party game gone wrong? Time to investigate.

1

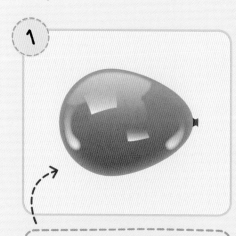

Blow the balloon up until it's about the size of a grapefruit.

2

Pinch the balloon shut, but don't tie it.

3

Rub some water on the rims of six plastic cups.

4

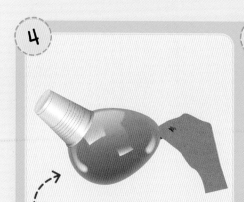

Press the rim of a cup tightly against the side of the balloon and then remove your hand. The cup should stay in place.

5

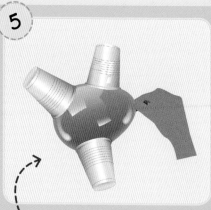

Try sticking on one or two more cups in the same way.

6

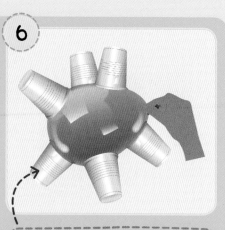

Blow up the balloon a little more, wet more cups and add them one by one.

HOW DOES IT WORK?

This experiment is an exploration of air pressure and surface tension. First of all, the wet surface of the rims helped the cups stick to the surface of the balloon because of a force called surface tension. Inside was one "cupful" of air. As you inflated the balloon more, the surface of the balloon flattened a little, so that the trapped air took up more volume (space) in the cup. This meant the trapped air lost some of its pressure. But the outside air pressure remained the same, forcing the cups against the balloon.

TOP TIP!

It's easier to do this experiment if you have a friend to help you—perhaps pressing the cups while you blow the balloon.

WHAT HAPPENS IF...?

Lots of science experiments work if you "scale up" or "scale down"—using larger or smaller ingredients to achieve the same result. Can you imagine trying this experiment at the beach, using a beach ball and some plastic buckets? Where else can you imagine performing a version of this experiment?

REAL-LIFE SCIENCE

Have you ever stood in sticky mud and found that your boots seemed to be locked in the mud—or even stayed put as you moved on? That's the power of air pressure! There was little or no air below your boot to press up, but the air pressure all around the boot still pressed down.

Falling Prices

Everyone has piled into your family car, buckled up, and then off you go. It's not as if one of you is left behind as the car drives off, is it? So a coin resting on a playing card will be the "passenger" if you give that card a flick. Right? Hmmm. Maybe not.

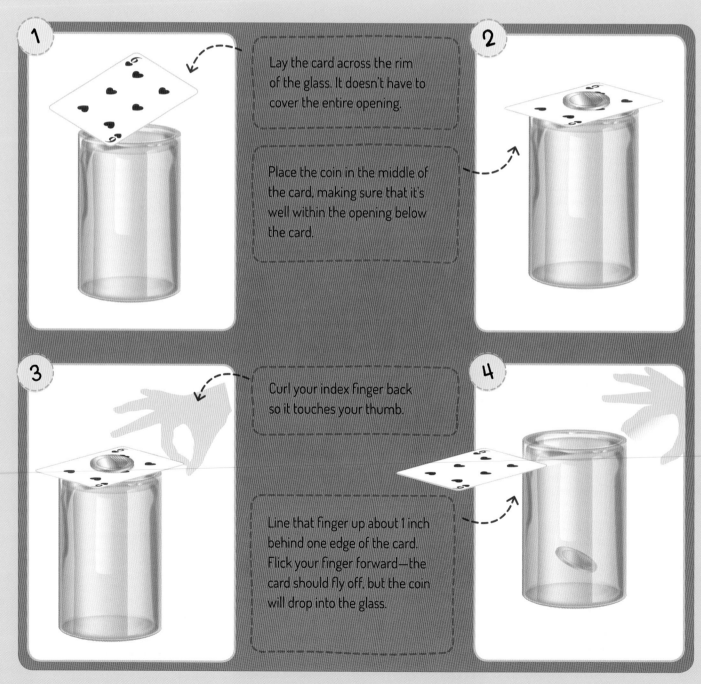

1

Lay the card across the rim of the glass. It doesn't have to cover the entire opening.

2

Place the coin in the middle of the card, making sure that it's well within the opening below the card.

3

Curl your index finger back so it touches your thumb.

4

Line that finger up about 1 inch behind one edge of the card. Flick your finger forward—the card should fly off, but the coin will drop into the glass.

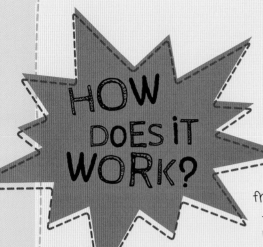

HOW DOES IT WORK?

This experiment is an excellent demonstration of Newton's First Law of Motion, which states that an object will stay at rest or will continue moving unless an outside force acts on it. That "unwillingness to move" (or the unwillingness to slow down if it's already moving) is called inertia. And it increases as something gets more mass. If you moved the card slowly, the force of that movement wouldn't overcome the force of the friction holding the coin in place. The much greater force of the flick overcomes the friction, so the object with less inertia (the less massive card) moves, but the coin doesn't.

TOP TIP!

This experiment works best with a glass glass, if you see what we mean. That "ping" when the coin falls in is a great payoff.

WHAT HAPPENS IF...?

Can you imagine setting a table with crystal glasses and fine china, and then whisking the tablecloth quickly from beneath everything? This classic magic trick uses the same principle as your experiment, and nothing breaks! But it takes a lot of practice to master this trick, so it's best to stick to coins and playing cards for now.

REAL-LIFE SCIENCE

You can see and feel the effects of Newton's First Law all the time. If you're in a car that stops suddenly, your body moves forward. That's why we wear seat belts. And if the same car moves forward suddenly, you feel pressed back into the seat. They're both examples of inertia.

Arch Power

You and your friends can build a medieval cathedral in your kitchen in a matter of minutes. Well, not exactly build a cathedral, but you can demonstrate one of the most important engineering features that has kept cathedrals standing for centuries. It's all about arches.

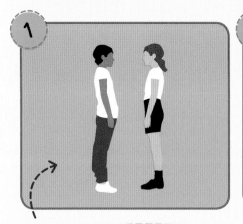

1

Have two friends face each other, standing and just wearing socks (not shoes).

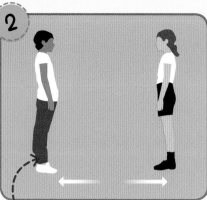

2

Have them take one pace back.

3

Ask each of the other friends to sit on the floor behind the first pair, so that their backs are touching the backs of the first pair's legs. (The second pair can still wear shoes.)

4

Ask the first pair to keep their feet in place and to hold their arms up.

5

Have them lean forward so that their hands meet. They are now forming an arch.

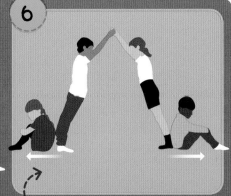

6

Ask the sitting pair to describe whether they can feel the force pushing out from the arch.

16

HOW DOES IT WORK?

The seated pair should have felt the force of the others" heels digging into them. That's because the standing pair had created an arch, and an arch is an important way of transferring forces. It takes the force of its own weight and any weight pressing on it (like the roof of a building) and transfers it into an outward and downward force along its curves. That's the force that the seated pair can feel, pressing out from the heels of the two friends standing. Engineers call the supports at the base of arches (the seated pair) buttresses.

TOP TIP!

It works best if the sitting pair keeps their shoes on to act as brakes against sliding (and to concentrate the force on their backs).

WHAT HAPPENS IF...?

With your four friends demonstrating how an arch works, you could work out how strong it is by measuring how much force it can transfer before breaking. Ask the standing pair to form fists before making an arch, then add book after book on to the level space along the back of their hands.

REAL-LIFE SCIENCE

Builders and engineers working nearly a thousand years ago used the principle of the arch as they built great cathedrals. At first, they built thick buttresses against the outside walls. Then they realized that even the buttresses could be arch-shaped to do their job. Those supports are called flying buttresses.

Low PresSure Affront

How much does a plastic bag weigh? Could you pick one up? If you think this is a trick question... it is! You can use some simple science to lock a plastic bag inside a bowl, or at least that's what seems to happen.

YOU WILL NEED

- Large kitchen mixing bowl
- Plastic bag (its mouth must fit over the bowl)
- Strong elastic band
- 1 or more friends

1

Open the bag and use it to line the inside of the bowl.

2

Press it snugly down and fold the spare plastic over the rim of the bowl.

3

Secure this outer plastic to the bowl with the elastic band.

4

Hold the bowl and ask a friend to pinch the middle of the bag and pull it out of the bowl. It should be very difficult, or impossible.

HOW DOES IT WORK?

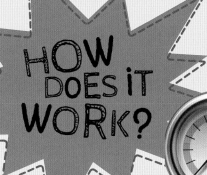

You've just demonstrated Boyle's Law. This scientific principle is all about volume and pressure. It tells us that if the same amount of gas (measured in the amount of molecules) is forced into less volume, or space, then its pressure increases. So, if the volume increases, the pressure goes down. That's what happens here when your friend pulls on the bag. Even a little tug increases the volume, and lowers the air pressure inside the bag. But the air pressure all around you hasn't changed. And it wins the battle of the pressures, holding the bag down.

TOP TIP!

It doesn't matter whether you use a ceramic or metal bowl, as long as it's sturdy. You don't want the strength of the band to squeeze the bowl out of shape.

REAL-LIFE SCIENCE

WHAT HAPPENS IF...?

So it's the outside air, which hasn't lost any pressure, that wins this battle. What do you suppose would happen if you used a much bigger bowl and bag? Or a smaller pair? Think about how scientists might measure the pressure exerted over a particular area, and you might find it easier to predict.

You've probably seen people blow up an empty plastic or paper bag, twist it shut and then slam down with their palm to burst it with a loud pop. That's another example of Boyle's Law. The air (a gas) inside got squeezed into a smaller volume and built up pressure—until it burst the bag open.

Crater Making

You've seen images of the surface of the Moon (and some planets, such as Mercury). They're covered with craters of all sizes. Have you ever wondered what creates them, or why they're not all the same size? Time for some space exploration—in your kitchen!

1
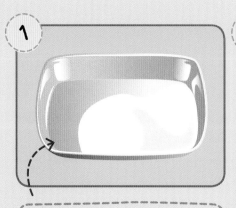

Pour flour into the baking pan and shake it until you have an even layer on the base, about ¼ inch thick.

2

Sprinkle the cocoa mix or instant coffee to make a light layer over the flour.

3
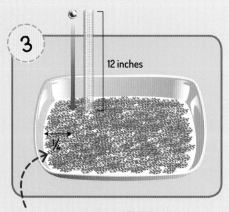

Hold the smallest marble 12 inches above the pan (using the ruler to be accurate), one quarter of the way in from one side.

4
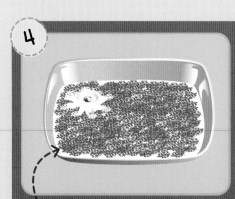

Drop the marble so that it lands and makes a crater.

5
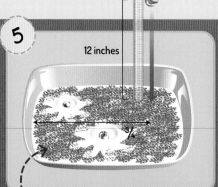

Repeat steps 3 and 4 with a second and a third marble—one over the middle of the pan, and one three-quarters of the way in from the same side.

6

Measure the depth and width of each crater.

HOW DOES IT WORK?

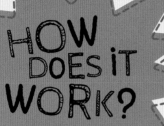

Newton's Second Law of Motion deals with force, the mass of an object and its acceleration. But acceleration isn't always about speeding up—it can also be about slowing down. And that's what these three marbles are doing. They're each slowing down from falling speed to zero, so the acceleration is the same. The big difference is in their size, or mass. And Newton's Law says that Force is made up of Mass times Acceleration (F=MA). So the bigger the mass in this experiment, the larger the force—and the bigger the crater.

TOP TIP!

If you use instant coffee, it's better if you can use powder and not granules.

WHAT HAPPENS IF...?

You can see—and measure—the various crater sizes caused by the different marbles. And it's clear that the marble with the greatest mass created the largest crater. Now think about the shape and size of the marbles. Would a flat, wider object, such as a domino, create a larger crater than a marble of the same mass? Maybe you can see for yourself.

REAL-LIFE SCIENCE

The surface of the Moon is covered in craters, caused by meteors crashing into it. Why isn't the Earth also covered in craters? Well, there are some, where huge meteors hit our planet. But most meteors burn up in our atmosphere—the friction of passing through the gases destroys them. The Moon has no atmosphere, so it has lots of craters.

Take a Pen for Spin

How do you get a pen to stay upright without holding it? One way, of course, is to tuck it into the sort of pen stand that stores multiple pens. Or you could use a bit of science—and a bit of a twist—to keep it balanced on nothing more than its own tip.

1

Hold the pen upright, so that its tip just touches the floor or table.

2

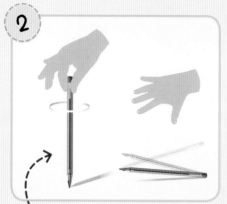

Spin it with a quick twist of your fingers, as if you were getting a spinning top started. The pen will fall right over.

3

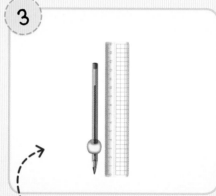

Wrap a piece of sticky tack (about twice the size of a pea) around the pen, about 1 inch up from the tip.

4

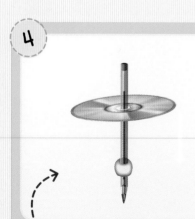

Slide the DVD on to the pen and press it down firmly on to the sticky tack.

5

Now repeat steps 1 and 2, holding the pen upright and then spinning it like a top.

6

See how long the pen spins for this time.

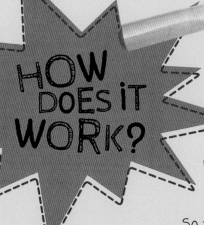

HOW DOES IT WORK?

You've just been demonstrating a scientific principle called angular momentum. "Momentum" describes the strength of a moving object. It's a combination of its mass and its velocity. A baseball bat (lots of mass) has more momentum than a cardboard tube (not much mass) swung at the same speed. Angular momentum describes the strength of spinning objects. It also multiplies mass by velocity, and multiplies that by the radius, or how far out the object extends from the spinning center. Including the DVD and sticky tack added mass, and the width of the DVD lengthened the radius. So the angular momentum increased, and the pen stayed upright.

TOP TIP!

Before you spin the pen the second time, hold it upright near the floor and make sure that the DVD is parallel to the floor. Adjust it if it's not.

WHAT HAPPENS IF...?

What if you hunted around in your parents' music collection and found a vinyl LP record? You could do the same experiment, but you'd need a bit more sticky tack, because a record is heavier than a DVD. The angular momentum would increase even more, and the pen would spin even longer.

REAL-LIFE SCIENCE

You've probably noticed angular momentum on bikes already, even if you didn't know the scientific term. Have you noticed that a bigger bicycle is steadier than a smaller one going the same speed? That's because the radius of the bigger bike's wheel is larger.

Prepare for Takeoff

YOU WILL NEED

- 2 long, slim party balloons
- Scissors · Ruler
- 80 feet clear fishing line
- 2 lengths of drinking straw (each 1 inch long)
- Empty 1-liter plastic bottle
- Masking tape
- A friend

How many times have you heard people say, "Well, it's not rocket science, is it?" This is a great experiment that really is about rocket science. Just make sure you have somewhere large enough outside so that you can say "Mission accomplished!"

1

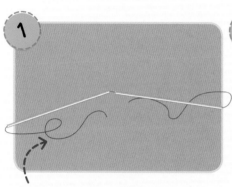

Thread the two lengths of drinking straw on the fishing line.

2

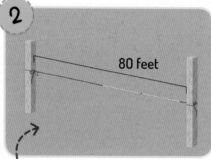

80 feet

Tie the fishing line between two strong objects, such as trees or tall fence posts. Make sure the line is taut.

3

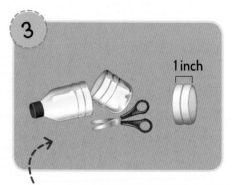

1 inch

Cut a ring of plastic, 1 inch wide, from the middle of the plastic bottle.

4

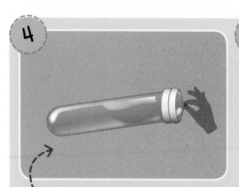

Blow up one of the balloons and pinch it shut; then press this pinched end into the plastic ring.

5

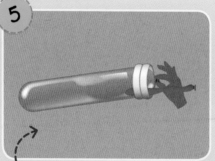

Press the pinched end of the first balloon against the ring while you insert the second balloon partway through the ring.

6

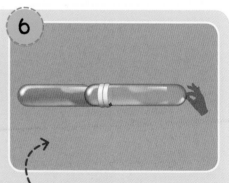

Now blow up the second balloon. Let go of the first balloon when it has been pressed firmly to the inside of the ring by the second balloon. Pinch the end of the second balloon.

7

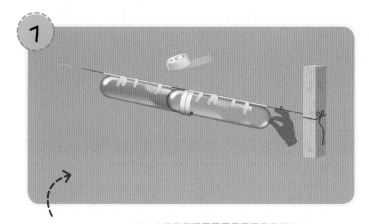

Have your friend attach each balloon to a drinking straw on the line. The straws should slide freely along it. Pull the balloon combination to the end of the line.

8

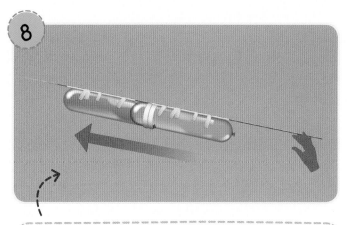

Let go of the balloon and watch your rocket zoom along the line!

9

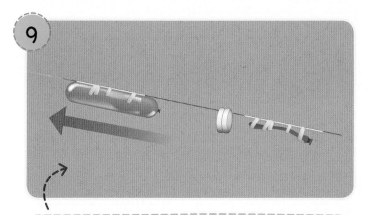

Partway down the line, the first stage (the second inflated balloon) should be discarded.

Take care when hanging up taut fishing line; people may not see it and hurt themselves.

HOW DOES IT WORK?

OK, you seem to have mastered rocket science, but how exactly? It's all down to Newton's Third Law of Motion, which tells us that for every action there is an opposite and equal reaction. Letting go of the balloon means that the high-pressure air inside it rushes out of the back of the balloon. And that motion, or "action," causes an opposite "reaction": the force that sends the balloon forward. The release of air from that first balloon also weakens its grip on the end of the second balloon, so the same action-reaction takes place a second time.

Continued →

TOP TIPS!

When you walk the rocket back to one end of the line, make sure the pinched ends of the balloon are pointing backward, so the rocket will go forward!

This experiment works best if the fishing line is very taut and also level. This reduces friction along the track, letting the stages travel further.

WHAT HAPPENS IF...?

If you had enough hands—and friends—do you think you could build a three-stage rocket? After all, the missions to send astronauts to the Moon had three-stage rockets. How would you work out which balloon should be the second, and which one the third stage?

REAL-LIFE SCIENCE

Well, as you've just built a rocket, you won't be surprised that space rockets work on the same basic principle as your model. Of course, they use special fuels such as liquid nitrogen instead of "balloon power," but they still rely on Newton's Laws of Motion. Your next stop—Mars?

Electricity and Magnetism

Become an even brighter spark than you already are, as you master the hidden power of electricity and magnetism at your fingertips and all around you.

Power a light bulb with a balloon (p. 32)!

Be a Tinsel Pilot

Jet engines, giant propellers, rocket fuel; these are some of the familiar methods of sending things into the air, and keeping them there. But electricity? Something sounds funny about an electric plane—unless it's the aircraft fuel of the future!

1

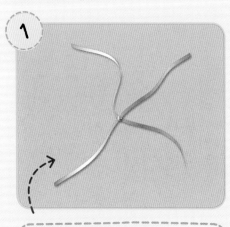

Tie the pieces of tinsel together about halfway along each length.

2

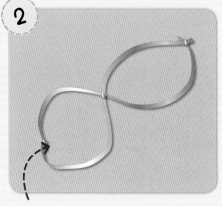

Loosely tie the four ends of tinsel in two pairs, so it forms a figure-eight shape. Blow up the balloon and tie it shut.

3

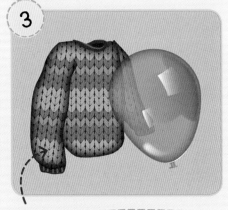

Rub the balloon vigorously against the sweater or scarf for about 15 seconds. Hold the balloon—rubbed side facing up—in front of you.

4

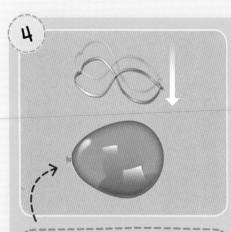

With your other hand, hold the tinsel above the balloon and let it drop.

5

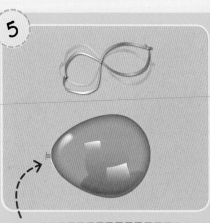

The tinsel should fall toward the balloon, then rise up again.

6

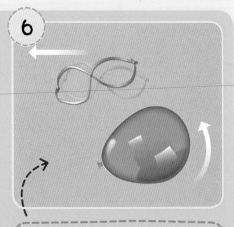

Keeping the tinsel hovering above the balloon, guide it through the air like a pilot.

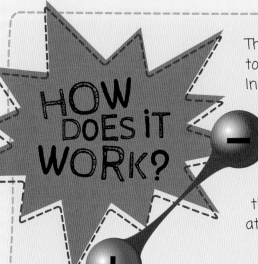

HOW DOES IT WORK?

This experiment is all about attraction—things being drawn toward each other—and repulsion, when they're pushed apart. In this case, we're talking about a slight electrical charge on both the balloon and the tinsel. Rubbing the balloon deposits lots of (negatively charged) electrons on its surface. The tinsel starts off with a slightly positive charge, so it begins to head toward the balloon. But lots of electrons jump from the balloon to the tinsel. Soon they both have a negative charge. What starts as opposites attracting, turns into like charges repelling each other.

TOP TIP!

If your tinsel doesn't rise, it might be because it has some plastic mixed in that cannot be electrically charged. If so, just use a single, shorter (4 inch) length.

WHAT HAPPENS IF...?

The force that's giving the tinsel its lift is electromagnetism, which has to do with positive and negative charges. But at what point will that force lose out to another force, gravity? You can test this battle by repeating the experiment with three pieces of tinsel, then four, and so on. How many do you think you can launch?

REAL-LIFE SCIENCE

Loudspeakers use a combination of a permanent magnet and an electromagnet (known as a coil). The permanent magnet sits inside a cone with the coil just in front of it. Electrical signals passing through the coil cause its magnetic field to shift back and forth, so that it's attracted to—then repelled by—the permanent magnet. All of this creates vibrations in the cone, and these vibrations create the sound waves that we hear as sounds.

The Electric Pencil

Some people refer to the television as "the flickering screen', and if you don't know why, try this simple experiment. You'll get an instant result, but the explanation takes a little longer to understand. Your audience might be happy to simply think of it as magic!

1

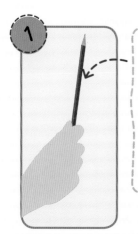

Ask some friends to sit facing a televsion. Hold up your pencil like a wand.

2

With the television off, wave the pencil quickly from side to side in front of the screen. Your friends should just see a blur.

3

Now turn the television on and repeat step 2.

4

Your friends should see several motionless pencils "stuck" in the path where you've waved.

HOW DOES IT WORK?

Televisions translate electrical signals into forms that we can understand with our senses. They produce sounds, but it's their image-producing that is a little more involved. What we see as moving images is actually a series of still images shown quickly. Electronic equipment scans the screen about 50 times a second. In this experiment, your hand waves the pencil quickly in front of the screen. At times the pencil is moving in sync with the flashing, so that the image from a single flash (with the pencil in front of that still image) lingers in your mind.

TOP TIP!

You'll get the best effects if your movement is smooth (even if it's fast), rather than jerky.

REAL-LIFE SCIENCE

The trick of "stopping" moving objects with quickly flashing lights is called the stroboscopic effect. It can be used in photography or filmmaking, so that we can see a tennis ball the moment it's served or a raindrop hitting a puddle. Engineers use this effect to check on quickly moving machinery while it is operating.

WHAT HAPPENS IF...?

You know that the flashing lights are sending you a series of still images, and that it's all tied in with timing your movement with the rhythm of the flashes. Try getting an adult to place a fan in front of the television and then run the fan at different speeds. If its blades are rotating at a multiple of the flash (exactly 40 or 50 times faster) then you might even see the blades stop. Why do you think that happens?

Funny Headlight

YOU WILL NEED

- Fluorescent light bulb
- Balloon
- A good head of hair
- Room that can be darkened when the lights are off

Don't be modest—you're pretty bright, aren't you? But are you bright enough to turn a light bulb on with just your head and no electrical equipment? The answer might surprise you, even if you haven't found a way of cutting all your parents' electrical bills—yet.

1

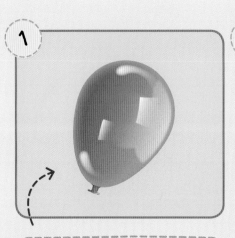

Blow up the balloon and tie it securely.

2

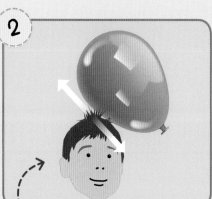

Rub the balloon back and forth quickly against your hair for about 30 seconds.

3

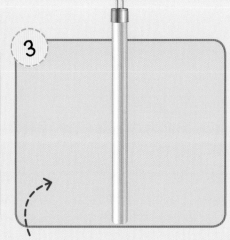

Hold the bulb vertically, with the two metal prongs facing up. Turn out the lights.

4

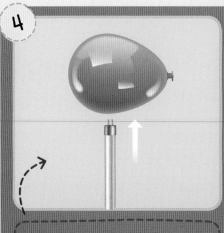

Touch the balloon (the side that was rubbed against your hair) against the prongs.

5

The light should glow noticeably while the balloon is touching the prongs.

Take great care holding the bulb; make sure it doesn't fall and shatter.

HOW DOES IT WORK?

Electrons can move from one object to another, either along a pathway, such as a conductive wire, or by "jumping." When you rubbed the balloon, you were causing some electrons in your hair to "jump" to the surface of the balloon. That side of the balloon took on a negative charge, because electrons are negative. They were then attracted to the metal prongs of the bulb and passed inside the gas chamber. That's where they bumped into atoms of the gas inside the bulb. The collision released photons, the basic particles of visible light. And that's what caused the bulb to glow.

TOP TIP!

If you don't have a spare fluorescent bulb, you could ask an adult to remove one from the ceiling for this experiment.

REAL-LIFE SCIENCE

WHAT HAPPENS IF...?

Imagine if you had the patience (and strength) to rub the balloon for two or even three minutes. You know that a thirty-second rub produced some light. Would the extra rubbing build up a stronger charge and make the light shine more brightly? Try to predict what would happen, and start rubbing!

You saw how a small amount of human "rubbing power" could light your bulb. So you won't be surprised to learn that fluorescent bulbs are extremely popular forms of artificial lighting. Older kinds of bulbs had to heat a wire until it glowed, which used far more energy than powering a fluorescent bulb.

The Bitter Battery

YOU WILL NEED

- Plastic ice-cube tray
- 80 ml of vinegar
- 5 uncoated nails (about 2 inches long)
- An LED with two lengths of wire
- 20 inches of copper wire
- Strong scissors or wire cutters
- Ruler

It's a hot summer's night and you've just lost power in a thunderstorm. Oh well, I suppose all you can do is open the freezer, find the ice-cube tray and use it to light the room. What?! Maybe not light the room, but it can shed some light on things. Here's how.

1
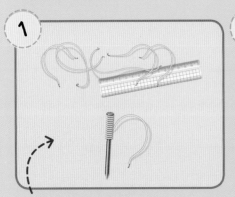

Cut the wire into five 4-inch lengths. Wrap a wire around a nail, starting just below the nail head, leaving about 2 inches unwound and sticking out.

2
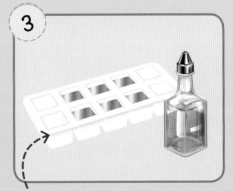

Repeat step 1 with the other wires and nails.

3
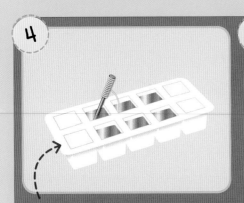

Fill six compartments (two rows of three) of the ice-cube tray with vinegar.

4
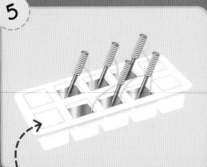

Place one of the nails in a corner compartment of the tray, with its length of wire placed in the next compartment.

5
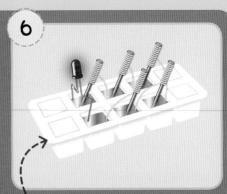

Repeat step 4 with all the nails. At the end you'll have the first compartment with only a nail and the last with only a wire.

6

Carefully place one of the LED wires in the first compartment and the other wire in the last—the LED should light.

HOW DOES IT WORK?

You've probably noticed that the pattern of nails and wires finishes up where it started. In fact, you could call it a circuit, just as racing cars go around a circuit. Yours is an electrical circuit of the type used in batteries. Household batteries place two different types of metal within a type of acid. You've added two types of metal (wire and nails) to an acidic solution (the vinegar). The flow, or current, of electrons in the circuit passes from a wire through the vinegar to a nail, then through the wire and vinegar to another nail, and so on. And the current is powerful enough to light the LED.

WHAT HAPPENS IF...?

Vinegar is a good conductor of electrons, which get moved along thanks to stored chemical energy. The vinegar's acid qualities help. Try using some other household liquids, such as lemon juice, water or water with salt dissolved in it. Which of them work, and which fail? Can you work out why?

TOP TIP!

Make sure that none of the nails are touching any of the wires.

REAL-LIFE SCIENCE

Batteries power so many things we come across in daily life, from cell phones and laptops to electric cars. Engineers are constantly developing batteries that will hold their charge longer or store large amounts of electricity derived from solar energy.

Potato Power

YOU WILL NEED

- 1 large potato
- 3 double-ended alligator clips
- Cutting board
- Knife
- 2 pennies (or other "copper" coins)
- 2 galvanized nails, each about 2½ inches long
- LED with wire leads

If you were planning to explore a deep, dark cave, the last thing you'd expect to pack would be potatoes and nails. But maybe you'd think twice if you knew what they had in store. They just might "brighten your day."

1

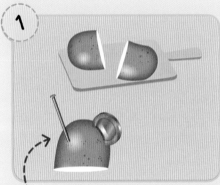

Cut the potato in half and lay the two pieces, flat side down, on a table or cutting board. Press a nail and a coin into one potato half, making sure they don't touch.

2

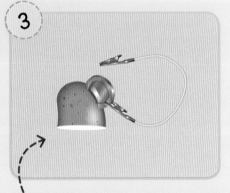

Attach one end of an alligator clip to the nail and one end of another clip to the coin.

3

Attach one end of the third alligator clip to the second coin. Slide that coin into the second potato half.

4

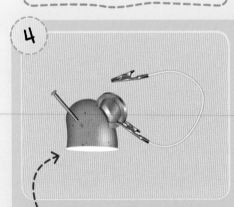

Press the second nail (with no clip on it so far) into the second potato half, making sure that it doesn't touch the coin.

5

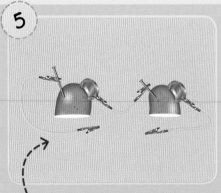

Use the clip to connect the "first" coin to the "second" nail.

6

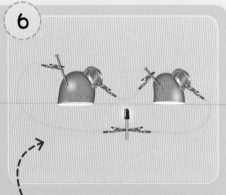

You should now have two unused clips. Attach each of these to one of the leads of the LED; it should light up.

HOW DOES iT WORK?

The potato contains a mild acid, which eats away at the zinc coating of the nails and releases negatively charged electrons. That makes the nails the negative terminal of the battery. The same acid reacts with the copper in the coins, absorbing electrons in the process. Losing electrons turns the coins into positive battery terminals. With one metal (copper) losing electrons and the other (zinc) gaining them, the balance has been upset. Electrons flow from one metal to the other to balance things out. That becomes the electrical current. And that same current flows through the LED, causing it to light up.

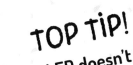

TOP TiP!

If the LED doesn't light up, attach the clips to the opposite wires. It's like putting a battery in the wrong way round.

WHAT HAPPENS IF...?

Other vegetables and fruits contain an acid that can help produce a battery. You could lemons, apples and tomatoes. See which of these works best and compare them to your potato results. The best way to compare is to turn the lights off just before you connect to the LED.

REAL-LiFE SCIENCE

This experiment calls for galvanized nails. Galvanizing is an industrial process that coats iron or steel with a layer of zinc. Your experiment worked because the acid in the potato reacted chemically to release electrons. Galvanizing is a way of preventing another kind of chemical reaction. It provides a protective layer so that the iron or steel can't react with oxygen in the air... producing rust.

On a Roll

You can understand some scientific principles more easily if you think of them as entertainment. What's at work might be complicated, but what you see is something fascinating. Need help understanding electrons? Get that can from the recycling bin and try this experiment.

1

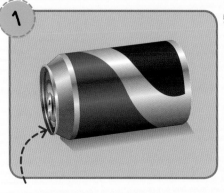

Lay the can on its side on a flat surface such as a smooth floor or a large table.

2

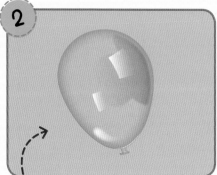

Blow up the balloon and tie it.

3

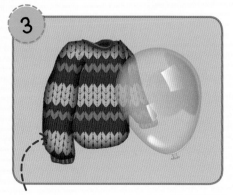

Rub the balloon vigorously against your hair or a sweater for 15—20 seconds.

4

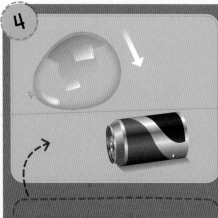

Lower the balloon carefully toward the can, taking care not to let them touch.

5

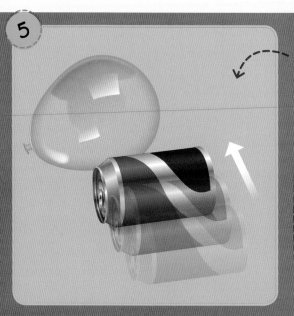

The can will start to roll toward the balloon. Get some practice attracting the can. You can even try to "lead it" across the surface, keeping the balloon and can the same distance apart as you move.

HOW DOES IT WORK?

This experiment—or more precisely, demonstration—is another example of static electricity in action. All matter, whether it's a sleeping bag or a pizza, is made up of tiny charged particles. Electrons, the negatively charged particles, can sometimes be drawn from one object to another. That's called static electricity, and it's what happened when you rubbed the balloon against your hair or the wool. The balloon picked up electrons, and therefore a negative charge. That negative charge repelled (pushed away) some of the can's electrons. When they escaped, the can gained a slight positive charge, which attracted it to the balloon. Remember: opposites attract.

TOP TIP!

You don't want to battle another force—friction—so make sure the surface is smooth. Carpets don't help.

WHAT HAPPENS IF...?

You can change the course of moving water with the same method. Rub the balloon on your head to charge it with electrons and then move it slowly toward a steady (but not too fast) flow of water from a faucet. You'll see the water change course toward the balloon.

REAL-LIFE SCIENCE

Static electricity is all around you. Your computer screen's slight electrical charge attracts dust to it. You might feel a shock when you touch something metal after walking across a carpet—static electricity again. But scientists and engineers can also use static forces productively, from catching particles in exhaust pipes to guiding ink to the paper with laser printers.

Magnetic Breakfast

Lots of breakfast cereals advertise their healthy ingredients. OK, so they're a good source of vitamins and other nutrients, but do they really contain iron—as in nails and hammers? Is there any way of telling? Well, there's one way you might want to try.

YOU WILL NEED

- Breakfast cereal—make sure that it says "fortified" or "contains iron"
- Cereal bowl
- Food processor
- Hot water
- Measuring cup
- Strong bar magnet
- Large zip-lock freezer bag
- Cutting board

1

Pour an average portion of cereal into the bowl.

2

Transfer the cereal into a food processor.

3

Fill a measuring cup with 250 ml of hot water from the faucet.

4

Pour that water into the food processor.

5

Run the processor for 30 seconds.

6

Pour the cereal mush from the processor into the freezer bag.

Continued

7

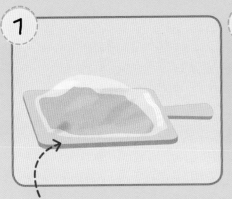

Carefully place the bag on the cutting board and slowly tip it down, making sure none of it spills.

8

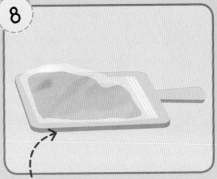

When it's on its side, with the air pushed out, seal the bag. It should be lying flat on the cutting board.

9

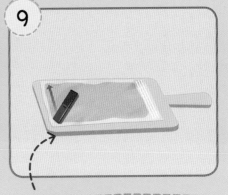

Press the magnet down on one corner of the bag and slowly push it across to the other side; keep the same pressure on it the whole time.

10

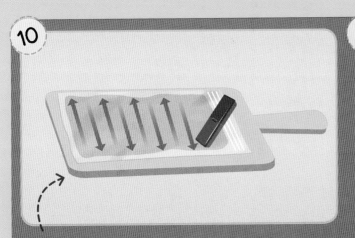

Keeping the magnet pressed down, work your way back and forth all the way to the other end of the bag—it should take a few minutes.

11

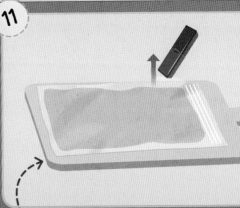

As you near the end of the bag, lift the magnet slightly. Some of the bag will probably stick to the magnet because of specks of iron being drawn to the magnet through the plastic.

TOP TiPS!

A white or lightly colored chopping board works best for this experiment.

If you don't have a food processor, you can pour the cereal-and-water mixture into the bag, seal it and squeeze until it's mushy.

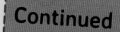

Cereal manufactuers can't just put chunks of iron into your breakfast. You'd probably choke! Plus, you wouldn't care for the taste. This means that the iron must be in the form of tiny specks. Normally these would be invisible, but mashing up the cereal made it easier to separate the iron from the grains in the cereal. And just as a chain of paper clips, attached to a magnet, starts to attract other paper clips, your tiny specks of iron gathered more bits as you went along. By the end, you might have seen a ball the size of a pinhead.

WHAT HAPPENS IF...?

You should have seen some results from this experiment—flecks of iron extracted from the cereal mush with your magnet. You could try the experiment without adding water. Do you think that you'd find more, or less iron that way? And what if you used cold water? Make some predictions and test the results.

REAL-LIFE SCIENCE

Iron is one of the most important nutrients—substances that help our bodies work best. It helps to draw energy from other nutrients and to keep red blood cells healthy and able to transport oxygen. We need iron from the food we eat. Some foods—like your cereal—have added iron in case you're not getting it from natural sources, such as liver and leafy vegetables.

Homemade Compass

Maybe you've heard of the Earth's magnetic north pole. Or that some long magnets also have ends that are called poles. Hmmm... is there a connection here? Here's a chance to find out, and at the same time imagine what it must have been like to sail the open seas without a radio, radar, or GPS.

YOU WILL NEED

- Sewing needle, about 2 inches long
- Bar magnet
- Cork stopper, ideally about 1–1½ inches diameter
- Cardboard
- Pen
- Ruler
- Sink or basin
- Water
- Glue
- Scissors
- Sharp knife

1

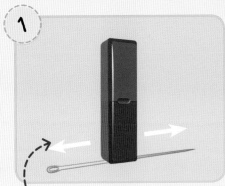

Hold the needle with one hand and stroke it five times in the same direction with the same magnetic pole.

2

¼ inch

Ask an adult to slice the stopper to make a ¼-inch-thick disk.

Be careful using sharp knives, scissors and needles.

3

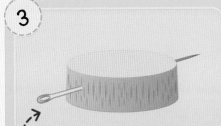

Push the needle carefully through the exact center of the cork disk.

4

Cut a circle from the cardboard, with its diameter just shorter than the length of the needle.

5

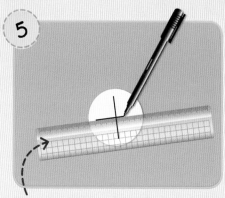

Use the ruler to trace two lines at right angles across this circle.

6

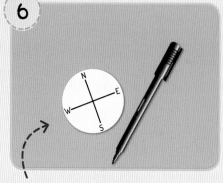

Mark the end of one line 'N" (for north) and the opposite end "S." The other two ends are marked "E" (on the right) and "W."

7

Fill the sink with water and carefully place the cork disk on the surface.

8

One end of the needle will be pointing north (see Top Tips).

9

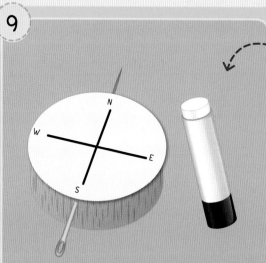

Glue the cardboard disk to the top of the stopper so that the "N" lines up with the "north pole" of the needle.

TOP TIPS!

In step 1, lift the magnet away from the needle after each rub, then lower it again to the end where you began for the next rub.

If you're not sure which way your house faces, remember that the sun rises in the east, and sets in the west.

HOW DOES IT WORK?

Rubbing the bar magnet against the needle "magnetizes" it, turning it into a magnet—at least for a while. And because magnets react with each other (think of how hard it is to pull them apart sometimes), your magnetized needle starts to react. It's reacting to an even bigger magnetic field: the one around Earth. And your magnetic compass lines up along the north–south line of that larger magnetic field. As you saw from marking your disk, once you know north, you can work out the other three directions.

WHAT HAPPENS IF...?

Eventually, your magnetized needle will lose its magnetic force. You can try different ways of making it last longer, though. Make some predictions to see whether rubbing a similar needle for longer will have an effect. What about using a stronger magnet to do the rubbing? See how the results match your predictions.

REAL-LIFE SCIENCE

If you're lucky, you can see the Earth's magnetic field in action. Northern (or Southern) Lights are like dramatic firework displays in the night sky. These displays occur when charged particles from the Sun reach the Earth's magnetic field. Some of them rush through the atmosphere near the magnetic poles. They react with gases to produce bright lights.

A Switch in Time

If you're trying to be environmentally friendly and save energy, you'll know enough to check all the light switches in the house. Here's a chance to let you "go with the flow" to see what happens when you click those switches.

YOU WILL NEED

- 2 metal paper fasteners (the type that look like thumbtacks before pulling their "wings" apart)
- Index cardboard
- Sharp pencil
- Paper clip
- 3 double-ended alligator clips
- 6-volt battery
- Masking tape
- Small light bulb
- A table
- 3 pairs of rubber gloves (optional)
- 2 friends to help

1

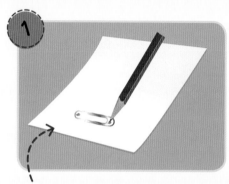

Lay the paper clip on the cardboard. Use a pencil to mark each end, just inside the paper clip loops.

2

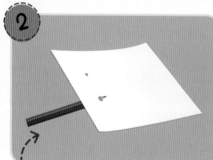

Use the pencil to poke a hole through each mark.

3

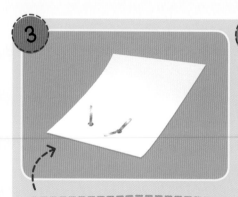

Push a paper fastener through each hole and then open up the wings of each fastener. This cardboard/fastener combination will be your switch.

4

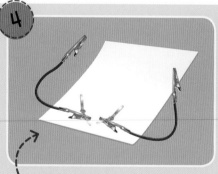

Connect an alligator clip to the wing of each fastener (one alligator clip per fastener).

5

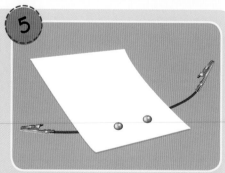

Lay the switch, unfolded wings facing down, on a table.

46

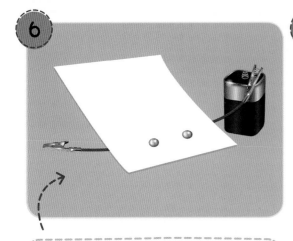

6

Attach the other end of one of those two clips to a battery terminal.

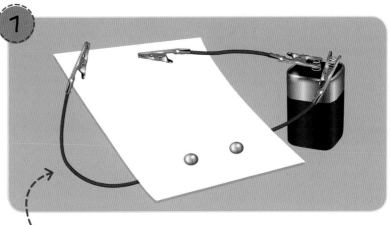

7

Attach one end of the third alligator clip (which hasn't been clipped to the switch) to the other battery terminal.

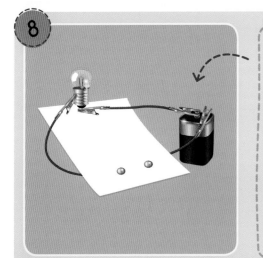

8

Have one friend hold the bulb. Touch one of the clips to the base of the bulb and the other to the metal side of the bulb. The light will not be on at this point.

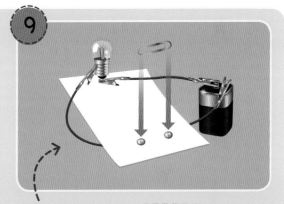

9

Have your second friend place the paper clip on the switch, so that it touches both metal fasteners.

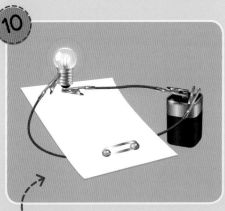

10

The switch has turned the light on!

If you prefer, you can wear rubber gloves as a safety precaution to prevent shock. However, the voltage of this experiment is very low.

Continued

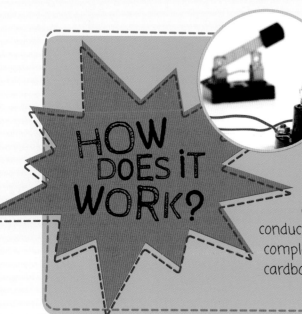

HOW DOES IT WORK?

You just created an electrical circuit! What's more, you showed what happens when that circuit is broken. Remember that electrons can flow from one object to another, provided that those objects can conduct the electrons (allow them to flow through). A circuit is just such a pathway, with electrons traveling along wires and through metal objects. The energy can power objects, such as the bulb. The paper clip conducts electricity, so the bulb lights up when the paper clip completes the circuit by linking both metal fasteners on the cardboard. And it switches the bulb off when it's removed.

TOP TIP!

You can save the bother of touching clips to the bulb if you use a bulb holder, which you can buy in hardware or science stores.

WHAT HAPPENS IF...?

If you had enough bulbs, alligator clips and helpers, you could add more bulbs to your circuit. Will all the bulbs shine as brightly? Try this out, making predictions and then recording your results.

REAL-LIFE SCIENCE

Every time you walk into a room and turn on the lights, you're using an electrical switch. In fact, you'll normally hear those devices described as switches even by people who don't understand electric circuits. This experiment operated on safe, low voltages but switches can become lifesavers when they are used to cut off power in high-voltage equipment.

Sound and Light

You're entering a world where things aren't quite what they seem. Did you ever think that you'd manage to slow the speed of light or make a dinner fork ring out like a gong? Prepare to be amazed!

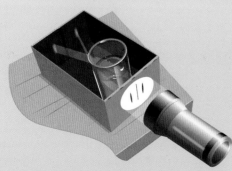

Measure the temperature of different colors (p. 54)!

Slowing the Speed of Light

YOU WILL NEED

- Shoebox
- Sharp knife or scissors
- Clear drinking glass
- Ruler and pencil
- Water
- Flashlight
- Table
- Dark room

Scientists tell us that the speed of light is as fast as anything can go—it's a speed limit for the whole universe! OK, so nothing can go faster than the speed of light. But could you make light travel more slowly? Time to find out.

1

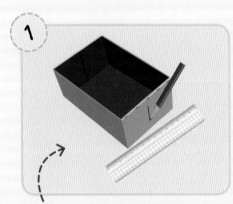

Measure the exact middle of one of the short ends of the shoe box and mark it with a vertical line.

2

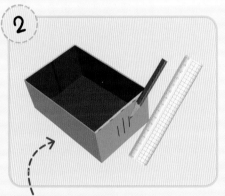

Measure and mark two vertical lines, each about 1 inch long, on either side of the first mark; the parallel lines should each be about ½ inch apart.

3

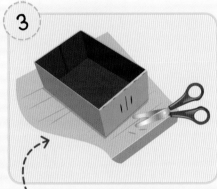

Rest the box on a flat surface, open side up. Ask an adult to use the scissors or knife to cut along the two outside lines. This will create slits in the box.

4

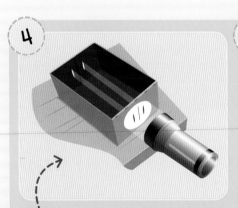

Darken the room and shine the flashlight through the slits; observe how the light passes through the inside of the box.

5

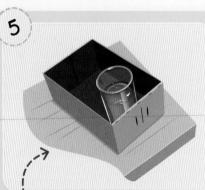

Fill the glass with water and place it inside the shoebox, just behind the two slits.

6

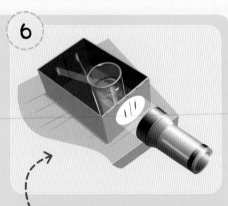

Repeat step 4.

HOW DOES IT WORK?

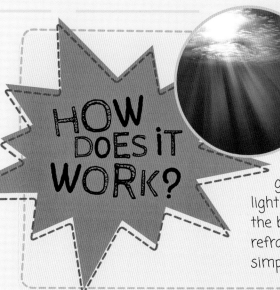

Light definitely has an upper speed limit, but there's no lower limit. Which means it behaves differently as it passes through different substances. Passing through just air, as in step 4, it seems unaffected, which is why the bands of light remain parallel. But light is slowed down, and its rays get bent, as it passes through water. You can see how the light changes direction—a process called refraction—in the way the beams of light cross in step 6. The amount that light is refracted depends on an object's optical density, and "optical" simply means "being visible."

TOP TIP!

Try moving the glass of water closer to, or further from the slits to get the best image of the beams of light passing through.

WHAT HAPPENS IF...?

You can test the optical density of different substances by changing this experiment several times. First, you can try it with different liquids: for example, does the light behave differently as it passes through cooking oil? Or warmer water? What if the sides of the glass were thicker? Try to predict how the light will behave in these different circumstances.

REAL-LIFE SCIENCE

Lenses are curved pieces of a transparent substance, such as glass. The amount of glass along this curve determines how much the passing light is slowed and redirected. Convex lenses are thicker in the middle and focus light on a point. Concave lenses are thicker at the edges and send light out like a fan.

TOP TIP!

Make sure that the circle of light from the flashlight is wide enough to cover both slots completely.

Sounding Off

What do your school gym, musical recorders, and some careful footwork have to do with microwaves or radios? Quite a lot, in fact, as you'll see in this great experiment. It calls for a large, unfurnished room, which is why your school gym (or similar setting) is ideal.

1

Mark half of the papers "loud" and the other half "soft." Give each volunteer some of each type.

2

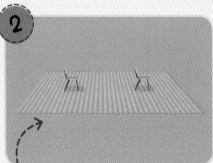

Set the chairs about five paces apart in the middle of the room.

3

Have the "musician-scientists" sit in the chairs and get comfortable—they'll need to hold a note for a long time!

4

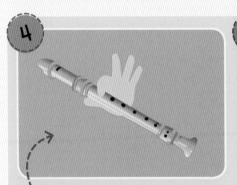

Ask each to play an identical note—for example, a B—and to hold it for as long as possible.

5

You and the other volunteers should walk around the room, listening to how loud the music sounds. Everyone will have to stop each time the musicians pause to catch their breath.

6

Leave a paper marked "loud" on the floor each time the music comes across strongly, and leave a "soft" piece of paper for the quiet sections.

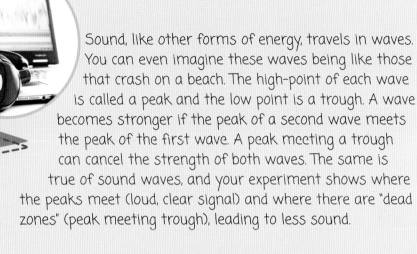

HOW DOES IT WORK?

Sound, like other forms of energy, travels in waves. You can even imagine these waves being like those that crash on a beach. The high-point of each wave is called a peak and the low point is a trough. A wave becomes stronger if the peak of a second wave meets the peak of the first wave. A peak meeting a trough can cancel the strength of both waves. The same is true of sound waves, and your experiment shows where the peaks meet (loud, clear signal) and where there are "dead zones" (peak meeting trough), leading to less sound.

TOP TIP!

It's important that your musicians play not only the same note, but also try to keep the same volume.

WHAT HAPPENS IF...?

Does this demonstration work in larger settings? The answer is YES. Concert-goers would be angry if some of the music were silenced by "dead zones" caused by wave interference. Special equipment, which measures the motion of sound waves, helps architects and engineers design the best size and shape of concert halls and theaters to avoid creating any "dead zones."

REAL-LIFE SCIENCE

Sound isn't the only thing that travels in waves. The same is true of light, radio, and all sorts of radiation. Have you ever wondered why microwaves have rotating tables? That's to make sure that there are no "dead zones" of uncooked food where the waves cancel each other out.

Red Hot—or Not?

Artists will sometimes call their favorite colors "warm" or "cool," but is there anything scientific about those descriptions? Imagine if you could measure the temperature of different colors. Well, you can—with this experiment. It's all about what makes up light.

YOU WILL NEED

- A prism
- Black tape
- Counter or table against a wall (must be near an outside window)
- Sheet of white paper
- Thermometer with liquid (not digital) display
- Pencil and paper
- Clear tape

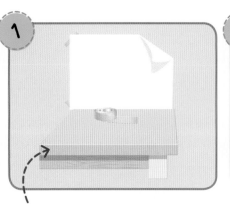

1 You want a clear, white wall for this experiment; otherwise you need to tape a piece of paper to the wall to create a white surface.

2 Cover the base (bulb) of the thermometer with black tape. This will help it absorb more heat, to create more dramatic results.

Don't ever look directly into the Sun, either with a prism or otherwise.

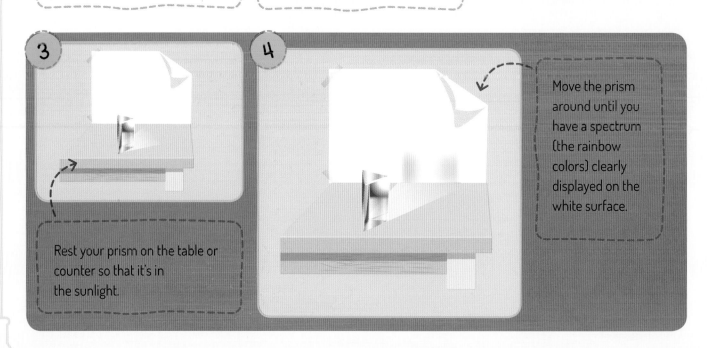

3 Rest your prism on the table or counter so that it's in the sunlight.

4 Move the prism around until you have a spectrum (the rainbow colors) clearly displayed on the white surface.

5

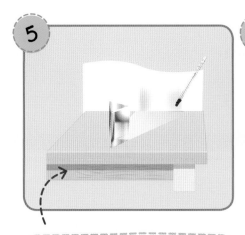

Lay the thermometer flat, jutting out from the wall, so that the bulb is in the blue section of the spectrum.

6

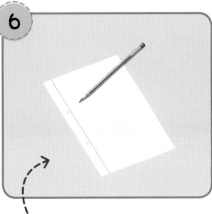

Wait a minute and then record the temperature.

7

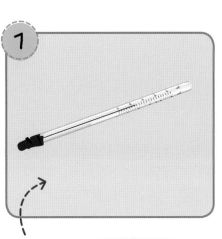

Take the thermometer away and let it rest for a minute.

8

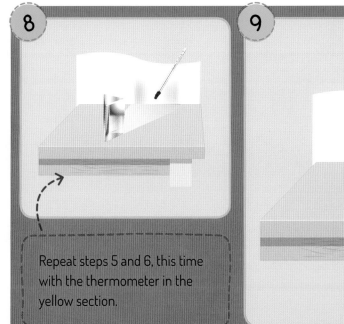

Repeat steps 5 and 6, this time with the thermometer in the yellow section.

9

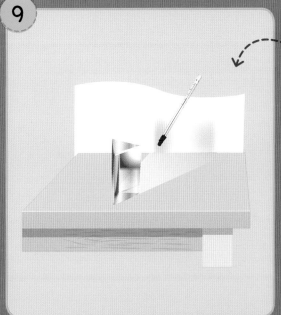

Remove the thermometer, rest it again and then repeat steps 5 and 6 in the red section.

TOP TIP!

This is pretty obvious, but you'll get the best results on a sunny day when the light is strongest.

Continued ➡

HOW DOES IT WORK?

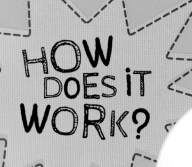

Sir Isaac Newton first demonstrated that what we consider to be white light is actually a combination of different-colored lights. The prism breaks the light down into those color "ingredients." The colors indicate the frequency of the light radiation—how fast the waves are vibrating. And this experiment also shows that the strength of that radiation—measured here as heat—changes according to its frequency (or color). You should find that the temperature goes up as you move from blue to red.

WHAT HAPPENS IF...?

Another great scientist, William Herschel, was the first to measure the temperature of the different-colored lights of the spectrum. He did something extra—which you can also try. You can take a fourth temperature reading, just as you did for the first three, but this time in what seems to be normal white just to the right of the red zone. Do you notice anything special?

TOP TIP!

The closer your prism is to the wall, the clearer the spectrum will appear— and you'll get better readings.

REAL LIFE SCIENCE

Newton's observation was important, and Herschel's observation of warmer temperatures to the right of red was the first proof that there are forms of light that we can't see. He had discovered—and perhaps you've measured—infrared light. This and other forms of "invisible" light are vital in medicine and used in many everyday objects, such as remote controls.

Lasting Impression

You've heard people say "That book (or film, or speech) created a lasting impression." That's just a figure of speech, of course, but you can create a real lasting impression with this easy demonstration. Plus, you'll learn a bit about how our brains process what our eyes see.

YOU WILL NEED

- Thick cardboard
- Pencil   • Ruler
- Scissors
- Small flashlight (about 2 inches in diameter)
- Invisible tape (it looks frosted when held up to the light)
- Room that will be dark if lights are off

1

Cut a piece of cardboard, about the size of a playing card.

2

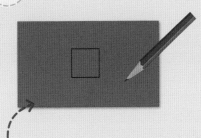

In the center of the cardboard, measure and draw a square with 1-inch sides.

Make sure the light from the flashlight isn't too strong. If your eyes hurt, opt for a weaker flashlight.

3

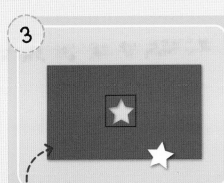

Cut out a shape—a circle, triangle, or star—inside that penciled square.

4

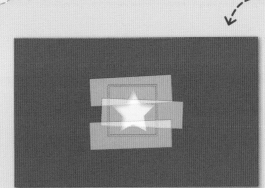

Cover each side of the cut-out shape with the invisible tape.

5

Turn off the lights.

6

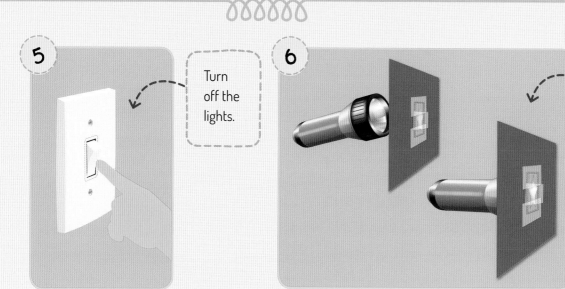

Place the flashlight against the hole. You can hold the cardboard, or tape it on to the flashlight to keep it in place.

7

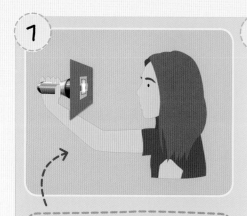

Hold the flashlight and cardboard in this position at arm's length and stare at the light for about 30 seconds.

8

Turn on the lights and gaze at a blank wall, blinking a little. You should see a dark image of the shape you were staring at in step 7.

TOP TiP!

Make sure that the piece of cardboard is big enough to block all of the light from the flashlight—except the light coming through the cut-out shape.

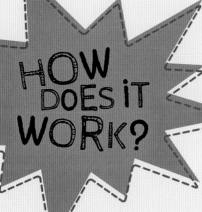

HOW DOES IT WORK?

The retina lies at the back of your eyes and is the area that is sensitive to light. The incoming light triggers chemical changes which the retina sends on to the brain. But the part of the retina that receives a strong light signal (for example, from the bright shape) becomes less sensitive. So when you look at the wall, it's that part of the retina that doesn't react to the incoming light. The result? A lasting impression of "no light," or darkness. That negative image eventually fades after about 30 seconds, as the retina readjusts.

WHAT HAPPENS IF...?

Wonder whether it's your retina or your brain that's playing this trick on you? Try the experiment again, but close one eye as you look at the bright shape. Then close the other eye (the one that's just looked at the light) as you look at the wall. You won't see a "lasting impression" because that retina hadn't been affected.

REAL-LIFE SCIENCE

Scientists are fascinated by the way that human and animal eyes work. Experiments like this one can lead to more complicated medical studies, especially on how photoreceptors (light-sensitive cells in the retina) help us to distinguish colors and to see in the dark.

The "Nuttiest" Sound

Here's a simple experiment that manages to explain the nuts and bolts—or at least the nuts—of how sound is produced and heard. It might be the easiest experiment in this whole book, but it links to many other scientific examples.

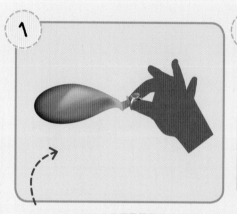

1 Carefully slip the nut into the balloon.

2 Hold the balloon by its narrow "lip" end and shake it lightly to make sure that the nut is all the way down.

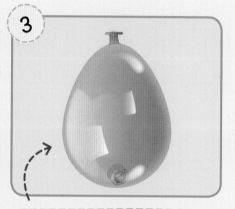

3 Blow up the balloon and tie it shut.

4 Hold the balloon by the knot, with your hand pointing down.

5 Swirl the balloon in a circular motion until the nut begins to race around the inside of the balloon.

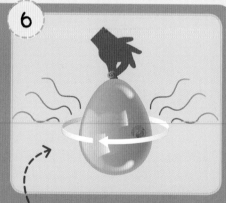

6 Listen to the weird, piercing sound that's produced!

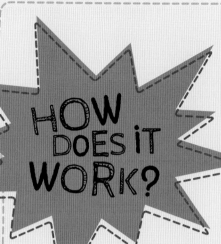

HOW DOES IT WORK?

With this experiment, you get two bits of science for the price of one! The first explains how it is that the nut races around and around the inside of the balloon. That's down to centripetal force, which pulls the nut inward and stops it from flying straight off.

The second relates to sound itself. The six corners of the nut tap the balloon as the nut speeds along. Each tap creates a vibration, which gets transmitted through the air as a sound. The individual sounds are produced so fast that it results in—what sounds like—a scary scream.

TOP TIP!

You may find it easier to swirl the balloon if you make sure the knot is in the palm of your hand, with your hand pointing downward.

REAL-LIFE SCIENCE

A satellite orbits the Earth using the same scientific force. Like the nut, it travels fast, and without the force of gravity pulling it in, it would fly off into outer space. The nut would also fly off its course if the balloon burst and it no longer pulled the nut inward.

WHAT HAPPENS IF...?

One measure of sound is its frequency—how often the waves of vibration are produced. Once you've got the hang of this balloon spinning, try getting the nut to travel faster or more slowly. Predict what you'll hear beforehand and then test your predictions (by listening).

Seeing sound

The world would be a pretty funny place if you could see sounds, wouldn't it? But is it such a crazy idea? After all, sounds are really vibrations that are picked up by our ears. So maybe there's a way of seeing those vibrations? Why not find out?

YOU WILL NEED

- Empty 2-liter plastic bottle
- Scissors
- Plastic shopping bag
- Rubber band
- Tea light candle
- Table
- Matches
- Ruler

1

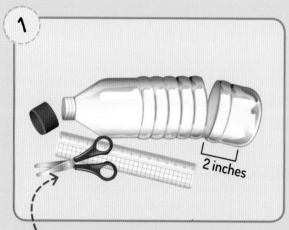

2 inches

Ask an adult to cut around the bottle, about 2 inches from the base.

2

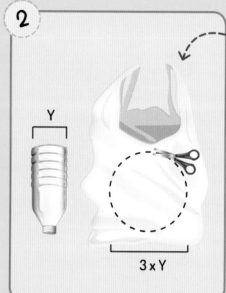

Y

3 x Y

Cut a circle from the bag that's about three times bigger than the widest part of the bottle.

3

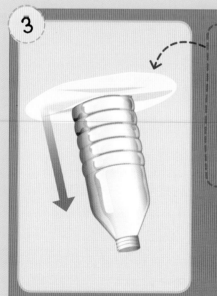

Lay that piece of plastic over the base of the bottle (the bit where you've just cut).

4

Stretch the elastic band over and around the base, so that it holds the plastic firmly in place.

5

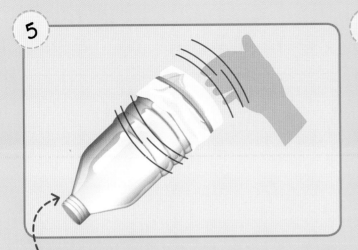

Tap the plastic lightly—you should hear a drumming sound.

6

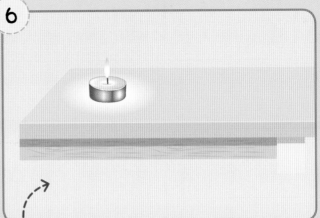

Place the candle on the table; ask an adult to light it.

7

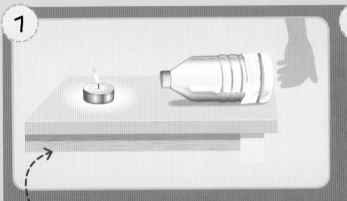

Point the narrow, open end of the bottle at the candle and tap the drum on the other end.

8

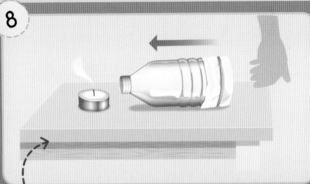

Move the bottle a little closer to the candle if it doesn't blow out.

Ask an adult to cut the bottle and light the candle.

TOP TIP!

If the plastic hangs too loosely over the base of the bottle, either double-up the band (to make it tighter) or use a slightly smaller band.

Continued

HOW DOES IT WORK?

We're pretty sure that you understand that sounds are really vibrations which are sent through the air. They're picked up by our ears, processed, and sent to the brain electrically. And that's when we hear those vibrations as sounds. Remember that those vibrations are actually waves. Each incoming wave at the seaside pushes you toward shore. The sound waves you produced, by tapping on the plastic, also had some "push." In this case, that force was enough to cause the moving air to blow out the candle.

WHAT HAPPENS IF...?

You can try the same experiment, but "scaled up," so that everything is bigger. See whether you can find an old (but clean!) plastic trash can and ask an adult to cut a large hole in its base. Cover that hole with plastic and rope—as you did earlier with plastic and rubber bands—and aim the other end at the candle. You should be able to extinguish the flame from much farther away.

REAL-LIFE SCIENCE

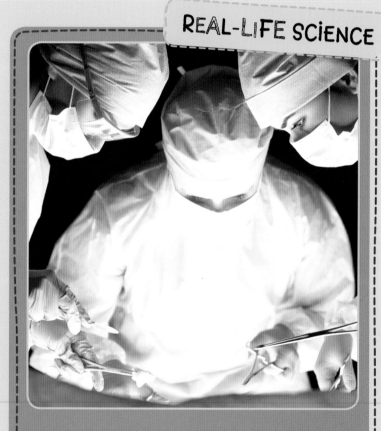

Scientists are constantly finding new uses for sound waves, and the force that they produce. By focusing the waves in a particular direction, they can cause objects to levitate (float) or move along a surface. Sound waves may soon provide a way of performing surgery without cutting people open.

Frozen Lantern

A scientific experiment should have a hypothesis—a kind of question or prediction about what will happen during the experiment. What do you think will happen to light as it shines through ice? Well... maybe it's time to find out, by seeing for yourself!

YOU WILL NEED

- An LED
- Two 15-inch lengths of thin, insulated copper wire
- Balloon
- 12-inch length of of string or a freezer bag clip
- Electrical tape
- Water
- Freezer
- 1.5 volt battery (AA is the best size)
- A friend

1

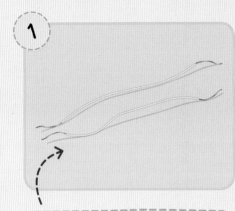

Ask an adult to trim 1 inch of plastic coating from each end of the wires.

2

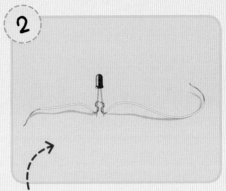

Attach one wire to each of the LED connections.

Ask an adult to help you with this experiment!

3

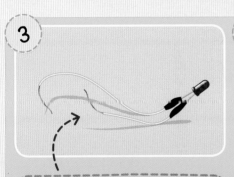

Tape around each connection securely.

4

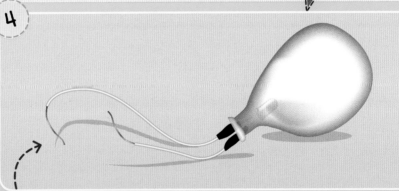

Slide the LED carefully into the balloon, with the two wires sticking out.

5

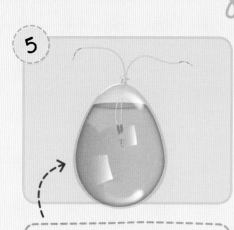

Place the neck of the balloon under a faucet and fill the balloon with water.

6

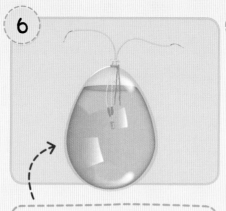

Holding the balloon upright, ask a friend to tie the neck tightly with the piece of string or clip.

7

Carefully place the balloon upright in a drawer of the freezer and remove again after 24 hours.

8

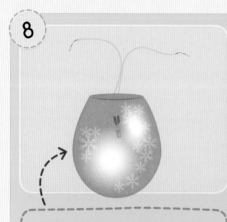

Carefully peel the balloon off the ice (using the scissors, if needed.)

9

Connect each wire to one end of the battery. Your lamp should glow with an eerie light.

TOP TIPS!

You might find it easier to blow up the balloon first and then let it deflate, before sliding the LED in (to give yourself some more slack).

You'll get the best effect if you can test the results in a darkened room—but make sure you're holding the balloon firmly.

HOW DOES IT WORK?

Hooking up the LED to the battery, of course, is a good demonstration of an electrical flow. But we're looking into just why it is that the result is so... spooky. After all, water is clear, so you'd expect to be able to look through 4 inches or so of frozen water (ice) to have a clear view of the LED. But ice is made up of many crystals, which reflect light in every direction. This is called a diffuse reflection. Tiny bubbles and particles locked inside the ice also contribute to this blurred reflection.

WHAT HAPPENS IF...?

What would happen if you used distilled or purified water? Both of these involve cleaning and filtering out impurities. What if you used ordinary water, rather than frozen?

REAL-LIFE SCIENCE

We come across diffused, or scattered, light constantly in nature. Just look up. A clear sky looks blue because sunlight hits particles of nitrogen and oxygen in the atmosphere, causing blue light to scatter more than other colors. And why are most clouds white? Well, they're made of ice crystals, which scatter light just like your lantern!

Dinner Gongs

Next time you're staying in a castle, you might be told, "our servant will ring the gong to announce dinner." That gong is probably about the size of a trash can lid, but imagine if you could get the cutlery to sound as loud (at least in your own ears). Maybe you can!

1

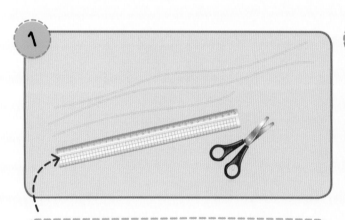

Cut two 20-inch lengths of string and one 12-inch length of string.

2

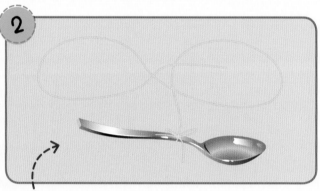

Tie one end of a long piece of string to the spoon, about halfway along its handle.

3

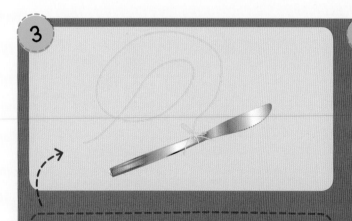

Tie the other long string to the knife, roughly where the blade meets the handle.

4

Tie the shorter string to the fork, halfway along its handle and with an equal length of string extending from each end.

5

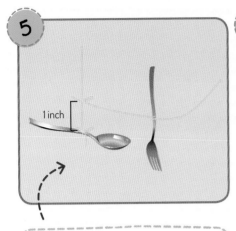

1 inch

Tie one of the "free" ends of the short string to the spoon string, about 1 inch up from the spoon.

6

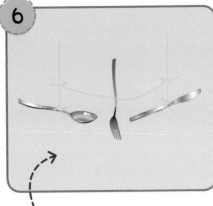

Repeat step 5 with the other free end, tying it 1 inch up from the knife.

7

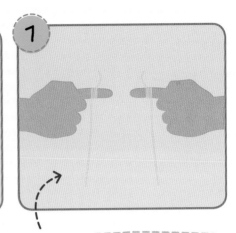

Bow a little and wrap the free end of each long string around an index finger. Press those fingertips to your ears.
The spoon, knife, and fork will be dangling below your head.

8

Shake your head back and forth two or three times.

9

You should hear a clear, bell-like sound.

TOP TIP!

You might need to adjust the strings to make sure the three pieces of cutlery hang at roughly the same distance below your head.

Continued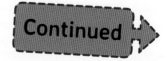

HOW DOES IT WORK?

Don't forget that what you hear as sound is actually a series of vibrations, which tiny bones in your ears detect. They then transform that vibration into a series of electrical signals that get sent to the brain. We normally pick up sound (or vibrations) that have traveled through the air. But vibrations can also travel through other substances, in this case along a string and your fingers, to your ears. Those vibrations have less chance to disperse and weaken (compared to traveling through the air), so you can hear the sounds more clearly.

TOP TIP!

You only need to shake your head gently to get the best sound; too much and the utensils will swing past each other.

WHAT HAPPENS IF...?

You can do a secret-agent variation of this experiment by tying paper cups to both ends of a much longer string, creating a home-made telephone. You can also test how sound travels through other substances. Call out to a friend when you're both underwater at a pool. What do you hear?

REAL-LIFE SCIENCE

You can see—or, more accurately, hear—how air can conduct sound differently. Blow up a balloon and hold it next to your ear. Listen to ordinary sounds, and they'll all become louder. That's because blowing up the balloon crowded the air molecules in the balloon together more tightly, which made them conduct sounds better.

Hot and Cold

Things will really heat up when you show some of these experiments to your friends. Even if they're too cool for school, they'll warm to these amazing demonstrations.

Make your very own pizza oven (p. 83)!

Water Race

Does your dad's face look flushed and red when he's been out for a run? There's a good scientific reason for that—and you can demonstrate it with just a few odds and ends from your own kitchen.

YOU WILL NEED

- 4 small glasses that can each hold about 5 fl oz
- 2 paper towels
- Hot water (from the faucet)
- Cold water

1
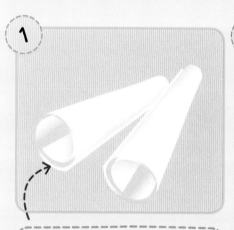

Roll each paper towel into a long, tight tube.

2

Fill one glass with cold water and another with hot water.

3

Place an empty glass next to each of the filled glasses.

4
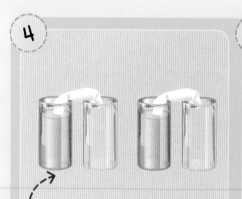

At the same time, rest one end of a paper tube in each filled glass and the other end of the tube in the empty glass next to it.

5

Observe which glass delivers water to its empty partner first.

You don't need to have scalding water for this experiment, but get it as hot as you can, within your comfort zone.

72

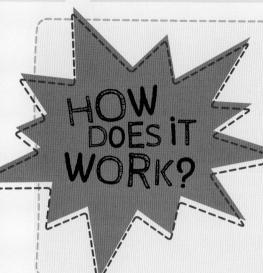

HOW DOES IT WORK?

The water travels through the paper in what's called capillary motion, taking its name from the tiny air tubes (capillaries) in the paper. The process, called osmosis, sends water from a denser solution (all water) into a less dense solution (the empty glass) via the capillaries. Heat increases the kinetic (movement) energy of molecules, so the warm-water molecules travel faster than their colder rivals. In both cases, though, the water is pushed upward by capillary action and then drawn down into the empty cup through gravity.

TOP TIP!

It doesn't really matter what type of glass you use, but clear plastic or glass gives you the best chance to observe the first drips.

WHAT HAPPENS IF...?

If you had enough time, what would happen after a few hours? That would give you the chance to observe another aspect of science: equilibrium. Eventually, the warm water would cool and the capillary motion/gravity seesaw would stop. All four cups would hold the same level of water.

REAL-LIFE SCIENCE

Your smallest blood vessels are called—surprise, surprise—capillaries. And when you (and your blood) get warmer—like after a run—those capillaries fill up with more blood (which contains water), heading out to cool down just under your skin. And you've just seen how the process works with your cups, towels, and water.

Heating Up

YOU WILL NEED

- 3 empty soup cans
- Can opener
- Sticky tack
- Masking tape
- 2 paper clips • Thumbtack
- Ruler • Pencil
- Printer paper
- 2 large books of equal size
- Table near a sunny window

Is there a connection between tomato soup and circling birds of prey? Well, with this experiment you can make that connection. It's all about convection, the term used to describe what happens when air warms up—or cools down.

1

Ask an adult to open the bottom of the cans and throw away the lids. Then ask them to tape the rim of each can with masking tape.

2

Pile the cans to make a tower, securing each junction with masking tape all around.

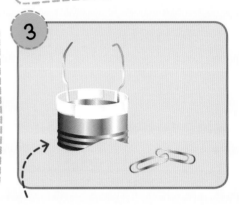

3

Straighten the paper clips and tape each of them to the inside of the rim of the top can, pointing up. They should be opposite each other and extending about ⅛ inch down inside of the can.

4

Carefully bend the free ends of the clips so that they meet and form an arch.

5

Strengthen this arch with a little tape where the clips meet, and place a small (pea-sized) ball of sticky tack on top.

6

Carefully press the thumbtack (pointing up) onto the sticky tack.

7

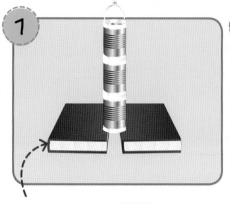

Lay the books on the table about 2 inches apart and set the tower over the gap, resting equally on each book.

8

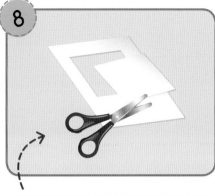

Cut the paper into a 6 inch x 6 inch square.

9

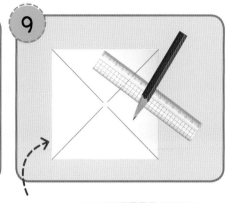

Use the ruler to mark a line from each corner of the paper toward the center, stopping each line ¼ inch from the center.

10

Cut along the lines you've just drawn.

11

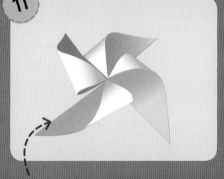

Bend every other corner of the paper down to the center and tape them all in place. You should have a pinwheel shape.

12

Carefully balance the pinwheel (taped side down) on the point of the thumbtack.

13

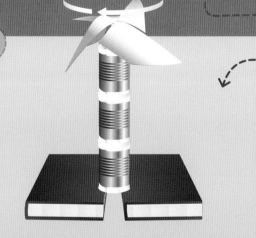

When exposed to sunlight, the pinwheel should start to spin.

Continued

Take care when handling scissors and pins.

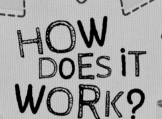

HOW DOES IT WORK?

You've probably learned that warm air rises. That's because the molecules making up hot air move around more freely and the air becomes less dense—and lighter. The sun shining on the tower heats up the air inside it, and the warm air rises up through the tower. Leaving the gap at the bottom of the tower allows more air to rush in, filling the space of the warm air that flowed up. It's the rising air that spins your handmade pinwheel at the top. This vertical movement of air is called convection. Cooling temperatures can cause air and other substances to sink—also because of convection.

TOP TIP!

Although you want the arms of the pinwheel held securely, it's a good idea to trim the excess tape at the joins to keep the arms lighter.

WHAT HAPPENS IF...?

Although this experiment works best on a sunny day with a window able to capture the heat, you could make some interesting observations on a day with changeable weather. Or you could observe the motion of the pinwheel each day for a week. Did you notice any difference in the speed of the pinwheel? Why is that?

REAL-LIFE SCIENCE

Convection plays an important part in how our weather develops and changes. You've probably seen those puffy cumulus clouds towering high into the sky. It's convection that fluffs them up like that. Hang gliders and soaring birds such as buzzards can capture updrafts to stay aloft, sometimes for hours.

Handmade Thermometer

Old-fashioned bulb thermometers have a column of mercury inside a glass tube. As things get warmer, the mercury expands and rises up the column. Markings alongside it equate to degrees. You can use a similar principle with good old air and water to make your own thermometer.

YOU WILL NEED

- Empty (plastic) soda bottle
- Plastic straw
- Sticky tack
- Water
- Food coloring
- Sharp knife

1 Half-fill the bottle with water from the cold faucet.

2 Add a few drops of food coloring and swirl the bottle, so that the water is evenly colored.

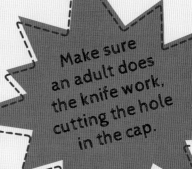

Make sure an adult does the knife work, cutting the hole in the cap.

3 Ask an adult to cut a hole in the bottle cap; it should be just big enough for the straw to pass through.

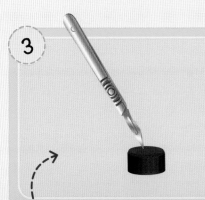

4 Screw the lid on to the bottle.

5 Slide the straw through the hole, so that the bottom is below water level but not touching the bottom of the bottle.

77

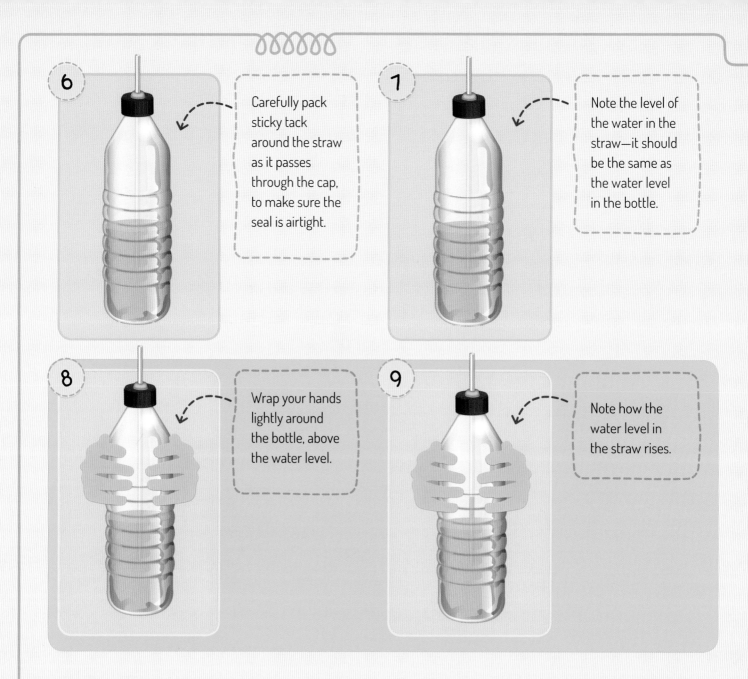

6 Carefully pack sticky tack around the straw as it passes through the cap, to make sure the seal is airtight.

7 Note the level of the water in the straw—it should be the same as the water level in the bottle.

8 Wrap your hands lightly around the bottle, above the water level.

9 Note how the water level in the straw rises.

TOP TIPS!

You can get a quicker, and more dramatic, result if you rub your hands together briskly for a few seconds before gripping the bottle. The friction will make your hands—and therefore the air inside the bottle—that much warmer.

You get the best results with a clear straw, but water that's darkened with extra food coloring will show through most straws.

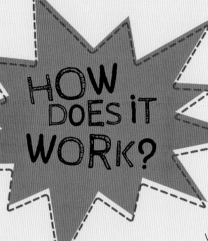

HOW DOES IT WORK?

As any substance gets warmer, the molecules that make it up become more active. And that extra activity—moving around more and more—means that gases begin to take up more volume. That's what happened here. Your hand warmed the air (a gas) inside the bottle. The air expanded and began to push on the water as it needed more space (or volume). That pressure, in turn, pushed water up the straw. The warmer the air, the more it expanded. And the more it expanded, the higher the water rose in the straw. Simple, when you think about it.

REAL-LIFE SCIENCE

Don't forget, you haven't created more air in this experiment. You've simply allowed it to expand. And if the same amount of a gas (such as air) fills more space, it becomes less dense. That means lighter, which is why the less-dense air in hot-air balloons provides all that lift.

WHAT HAPPENS IF...?

You can see how this experiment works by deliberately disobeying steps 5 or 6 in the instructions. If the straw doesn't extend below the water, the expanding warmer air simply escapes through the straw. Likewise, the air will find a way out if the seal on the cap has gaps—and your thermometer won't work.

Candle Seesaw

We've all had fun on a seesaw, and we've tried changing the speed by adding more weight or moving along one of its arms. It's pretty easy to work out how the forces we add (or remove) propel it. But a fire-powered seesaw? That has to be seen to be believed!

YOU WILL NEED

- Candle, about 6 inches long and 1 inch wide
- A long, narrow nail
- 2 identical drinking glasses
- Sharp knife
- Matches
- A table
- 2 saucers (optional)

1

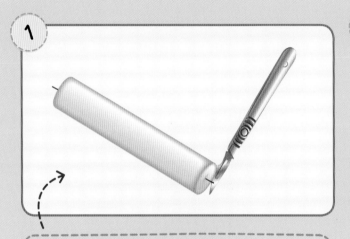

Have an adult scrape away some of the wax at the flat end of the candle to expose the wick.

2

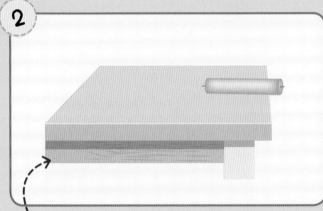

Lay the candle so that some of it juts over the edge of a table or counter.

3

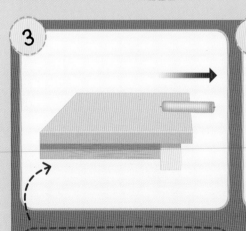

When the candle begins to tip off the edge, hold it in place.

4

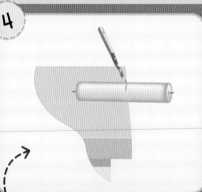

Ask an adult to mark the balancing point with the tip of the knife.

5

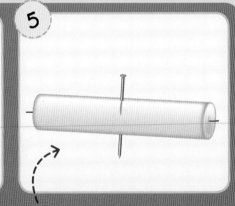

Get an adult to slide the nail slowly and carefully through the candle's balancing point, stopping when the same length of nail juts out on either side.

80

6

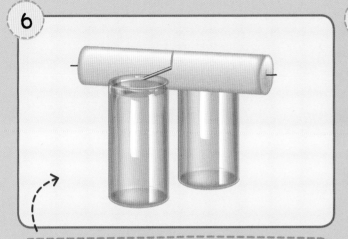

Line the glasses up side by side and balance the candle by resting the jutting nail on the glass rims. To avoid wax dripping on the table, you can place a saucer under each end of the candle.

7

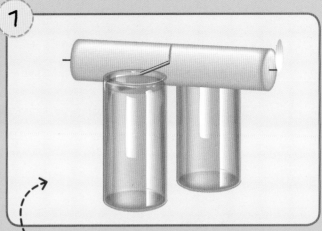

Have an adult light one end of the candle and then wait a few seconds until the lit end rises up.

8

Now ask the adult to light the other (lower) end.

9

Soon the candle will be moving up and down like a seesaw!

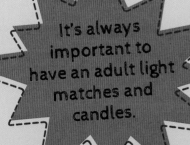

It's always important to have an adult light matches and candles.

TOP TIP!

Try to use a nail that somehow manages to be long and narrow, so that it juts out well, without breaking the candle.

Continued

HOW DOES IT WORK?

Although this is a simple demonstration on one level, a lot is going on. First of all, the reason we've grouped it in among the Hot and Cold experiments is that heat—an energy by-product of combustion (burning)—is the driving force. Oxygen from the air provides much of the "fuel" for the chemical reaction, and thermal energy (heat) is released. That heat melts the wax. And when some of the melted wax drips off, that end of the candle loses mass and goes up on the "seesaw." The other side burns more now, so that it loses more mass... until it swings up. And so on.

WHAT HAPPENS IF...?

If you're lucky enough to have a good supply of candles—and a patient adult with a steady hand—you could try using candles of different lengths. After all, you can change the speed of a normal seesaw by moving closer or further from the person at the other end. Do you think the candle length would affect this experiment? Test it and see for yourself.

REAL-LIFE SCIENCE

Heat and flames produce a rhythm in something that you know very well: cars. An electrical spark causes gas fumes to ignite (and expand) in cylinders inside the engine. The expanding gas pushes pistons up, and cooling gas lets them come down again. This up-and-down motion is fast and constant, and it provides the "drive" that moves the car.

the Pizza Oven

Were your eyes bigger than your tummy when you ordered that takeout pizza last night? Well, here's a chance to harness science—and solar power—to reheat those leftovers. Just make sure you do it on a sunny day!

Take care with the scissors when you cut the pizza box.

1

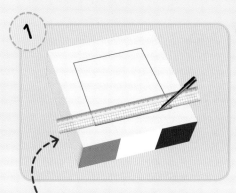

Use a ruler and marker pen to draw a square shape on the top flap of the pizza box, about 2 inches in from the four edges.

2

Cut along three of those four lines, leaving the line along the hinge of the box alone. Open and close several times to form a crease.

3

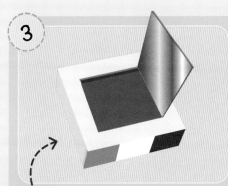

Cut a piece of foil the same size as this flap; glue it to the inside edge of the flap. This will reflect sunlight down to the box.

4

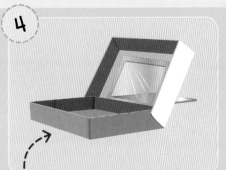

Cut a piece of plastic wrap just a bit larger than the opening. Use the packing tape to attach it to the underside of the box top, making sure it covers the cut-out hole completely.

5

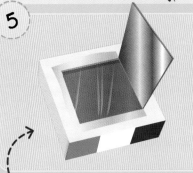

Repeat step 4, attaching the second piece of plastic wrap to the other side of the cut-out hole.

By now, the box top should have a seal, made of plastic wrap, covering the hole; the foil-backed flap should open up from seal.

6

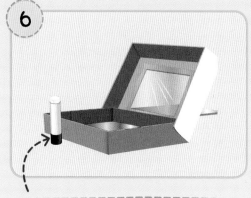

Cut a second piece of foil and glue it to the bottom (inside) of the pizza box. This piece will act as insulation.

7

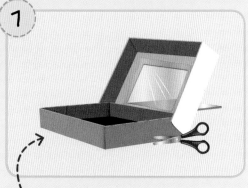

Cut some of the black construction paper to fit this same base; tape it to the foil on the base, where it will help absorb heat.

8

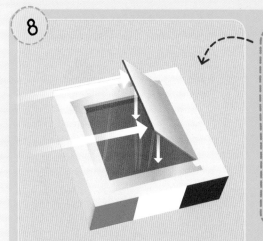

Aim the box so that it opens toward the Sun. Prop the flap open—but with the box top shut—to get the oven working.

9

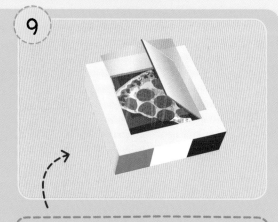

Place a piece of pizza in the oven.

10

Leave the pizza in the oven until it has heated through. You can heat up all sorts of things, provided they don't stick up higher than the box top. Marshmallows are particularly good!

Although this oven doesn't get as hot as the one in your kitchen, leave the flap open a few seconds before putting your hand in. This gives it time to cool a little.

HOW DOES IT WORK?

You've tied together lots of different scientific ideas with this one experiment. The main ingredient, of course, is the solar power—the heat from the sunlight. Some of it would pass straight through the clear plastic anyway, but the extra foil on the open flap focuses even more energy toward the base. The plastic allows energy to pass into the box, while preventing it from escaping. And black—the color of the paper on the base—absorbs more heat energy than other colors, with the lower layer of foil adding even more insulating help.

TOP TIP!

If you're lucky enough to have some sheets of PVC plastic—and an adult to cut them to size—you can use PVC instead of plastic wrap.

WHAT HAPPENS IF...?

You can easily see how this demonstration of solar power works by deliberately not following some of the instructions. With no foil on the flap above, the oven will have less fuel and the food won't heat as much. Try the experiment with just one element missing—for example, no foil above, the air seal not tight— and see how it works out.

REAL-LIFE SCIENCE

You've probably seen curved satellite dishes. Like your oven, they're designed to reflect radiation and direct it to a single point. Your "single point" is the base of the oven. A satellite dish has a receiver to pick up signals that have bounced off the curve and send them along cables to your TV!

ice Cream Chiller

YOU WILL NEED

- 2 bowls
- Ice cream
- Ice cream scoop
- 2 spoons
- Milk
- Volunteer (although you can do it yourself)

After all this disciplined scientific experimenting, don't you deserve a treat? How about a delicious bowl of ice cream—or better yet, two? Hmmm. We might even weave in a science angle, after all. Talk about a win-win situation!

1

Put two scoops of ice cream in each bowl.

2

Ask a friend to taste some of the ice cream in the first bowl, paying particular attention to how cold it feels.

3

Pour three or four spoonfuls of milk over the second bowl of ice cream; make sure you cover it completely.

4

Now ask your friend to repeat step 2 with the second bowl of ice cream.

5

Ask your friend to alternate between bowls, having a spoonful from one, then a spoonful from the other. You might need to take part in this experiment as well, if you haven't begun to do so already. Do you agree that the milk-coated ice cream tastes—or feels—colder?

HOW DOES IT WORK?

Things feel colder when they help transfer heat away from you. That's why metals feel colder than wood. We know that ice cream is cold, but it is also full of tiny bubbles. They're what give it that soft texture. But air is also a great insulator, which means that it slows the transfer of heat from one thing to another. Milk doesn't have all those bubbles. This means that the heat from your tongue or lips passes more easily through the milk (making it feel colder) than it does through the ice cream (with all those insulating bubbles).

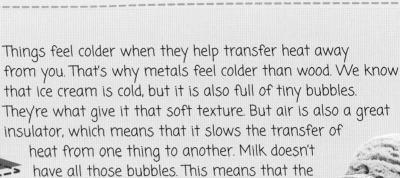

TOP TIP!

You can vary things by using different flavors, or use ice cream that has just come out of the freezer, compared to slightly melted ice cream.

WHAT HAPPENS IF...?

This experiment depends on the difference in consistency between the ice cream and the milk. What do you suppose would happen if you put some ice cream and some milk-covered ice cream back in the freezer? Try doing that, but use paper cups rather than bowls that might crack. Make a prediction, and see whether it works out.

REAL-LIFE SCIENCE

Farming villages in parts of Russia once held big celebrations when winter's first snow fell. That might seem strange, considering that their fields would be covered for the next six months or so. But the snow protected the crops underneath. Fallen snow is actually full of air, which means that the snow is really more of a blanket to keep the much colder air out. Under the snow it isn't exactly warm, but it remains a lot warmer than being in the bitter air outside.

Greenhouse Effect

Most scientists agree that the Earth's climate is changing, and it's a cause for alarm. Our planet has warmed—and cooled again—quite naturally over millions of years. But recent rises are most likely down to human activity. Why? Here's an experiment to help you understand.

YOU WILL NEED

- 2 identical drinking glasses
- Water
- Bag large enough to seal a glass completely
- Tape (unless you use a zip-lock bag)
- Thermometer
- Reading lamp (optional)

1

Fill both glasses almost to the brim with cold water from the faucet.

2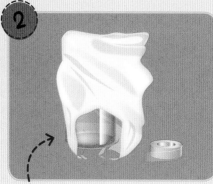

Carefully slide the bag around one glass, and seal it shut.

3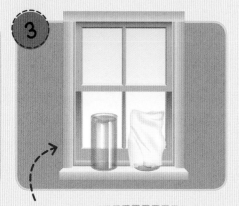

Place both glasses on a sunny windowsill—or about 20 inches below a reading lamp if it's cloudy.

4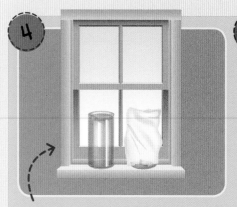

Leave the glasses for two hours.

5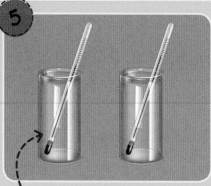

Undo the plastic bag and take the temperature of the water in both glasses.

6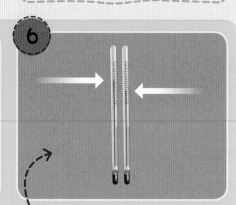

Note which water is warmer.

HOW DOES IT WORK?

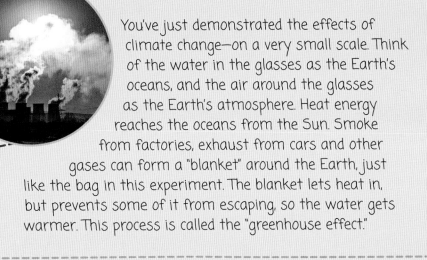

You've just demonstrated the effects of climate change—on a very small scale. Think of the water in the glasses as the Earth's oceans, and the air around the glasses as the Earth's atmosphere. Heat energy reaches the oceans from the Sun. Smoke from factories, exhaust from cars and other gases can form a "blanket" around the Earth, just like the bag in this experiment. The blanket lets heat in, but prevents some of it from escaping, so the water gets warmer. This process is called the "greenhouse effect."

TOP TIP!

Make sure the glasses are identical, so the results are more accurate ("glass" glasses work best).

REAL-LIFE SCIENCE

WHAT HAPPENS IF...?

If you have a period of changeable weather ahead of you, why not try the same experiment each day for a week. Does the "sandwich bag" water heat up even on cloudy days? How about trying the experiment with three different-sized glasses, each inside a bag: do they warm up to the same degree?

The effects of climate change are often measured in ocean temperatures. An overall rise of just 1°F might not sound like much, but it would cause a lot of damage. Some of the planet's ice caps would begin to melt, raising sea levels and threatening low-lying areas around the world.

The Fickle Flame

Sometimes you get a chance to show off more than one bit of scientific knowledge with just one demonstration or experiment. This is just such a chance and it's a good way to demonstrate how one principle can be affected by another. Confused? You won't be at the end of the experiment.

YOU WILL NEED

- Large table or other sturdy, flat surface
- Sticky tack
- Tea light candle
- Matches
- Glass mixing bowl
- Baking pan (large enough to hold the mixing bowl upside-down)

1

Roll a ball of sticky tack and set it in the middle of the pan to act as a candle base.

2

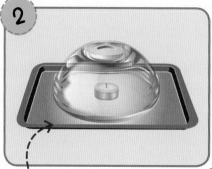

Set the candle on the base and place the mixing bowl, upside-down, over it.

Make sure an adult lights the matches and candle.

3

2 inches

Make sure that there's at least a 2 inch clearance between the top of the candle and the bowl.

4

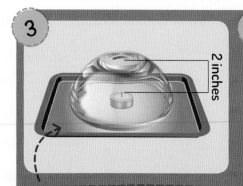

Remove the bowl and place four pea-sized balls of sticky tack along the rim, evenly spaced. They will act as soft bases when the bowl is overturned later.

5

Slide the pan back and forth slightly to make sure the candle is secure. Strengthen the base if it isn't.

6

Ask an adult to light the candle. Let the flame settle for a few seconds.

7

Slide the pan along the top of the table and note how the flame points backward.

8

Return the pan to the original position, with the candle still burning (or relit).

9

Carefully lower the bowl, upside-down, over the lit candle and make sure the flame is steady.

10

Repeat step 7 but observe how this time the flame tips forward.

You don't want the glass to become too hot, so blow out the candle after about 10 seconds.

TOP TiP!

You might need some practice in moving the pan quickly enough to get a reaction from the flame—but not so fast that the fire gets snuffed out.

Continued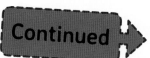

HOW DOES iT WORK?

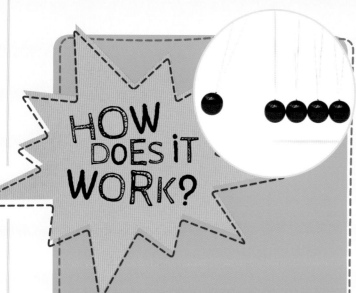

You've called on several different scientific principles in this simple experiment. Newton's First Law of Motion says that an object will stay at rest—or continue moving—unless an outside force acts on it. Moving the candle counts as an outside force, so the flame lags behind—when it's not covered. But covered, the flame heats the air near it (making it less dense). The other air inside the container lags behind (just like the flame the first time round). You can't see it, but it's bunched at the back of the moving container, pushing the hotter air (and flame) forward.

REAL-LIFE SCIENCE

You have experienced, or at least witnessed, both scientific principles at work here. When you're in a car that's setting off from a traffic light you feel pushed back for a while. That's called inertia, and it's inertia that "drags" the flame back at the start. Heaters cause the air of a hot-air balloon to expand and become less dense, which is what happened to the air heated by the flame under the bowl.

WHAT HAPPENS IF...?

Imagine if the "base" of the upturned bowl were much higher than the four pea-sized blobs of blue tack. If the candle burned long enough, warm air would eventually fill the bowl, pushing the heavier, cooler air out through the bigger gap below. What would happen to the flame if you moved the pan then?

Materials

Have you ever made something just disappear, apart from ice cream? Or conjured something out of nothing? You might manage both of these tricks with the experiments in this chapter.

Make a groovy lava lamp (p. 94)!

Lava Lamp

If there's anyone in your family—maybe your parents, or grandparents—who can remember the 1970s, they can tell you about lava lamps. Those fun lamps had blobs (the "lava") that constantly bobbed up and down inside a jar. You can make your own version with this experiment.

1
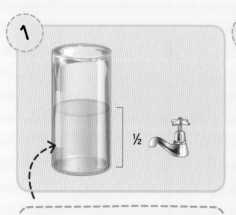
Fill the glass halfway with water.

2
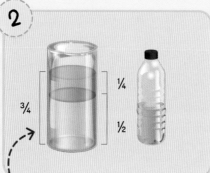
Slowly pour oil into the glass until it reaches about three quarters of the way to the top.

3
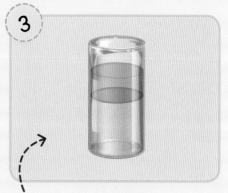
Wait until the liquids settle; they will form two layers, with the water below.

4
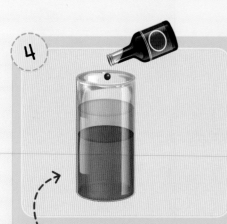
Add a few drops of food coloring—they will pass through the oil but change the color of the water.

5
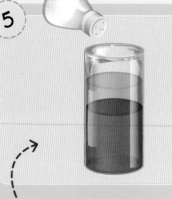
Shake some salt on to the top of the liquid and wait a few seconds.

6

Blobs of oil will sink to the bottom of the glass and then float back up from the water layer.

HOW DOES IT WORK?

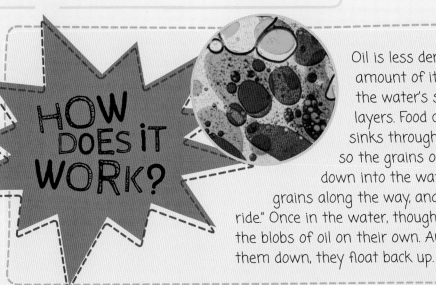

Oil is less dense than water (the same amount of it weighs less), so it floats on the water's surface. That explains the two layers. Food coloring is water-based, so it sinks through the oil. Salt is denser than oil, so the grains of salt sink through the oil and down into the water. But some oil sticks to the grains along the way, and the oil "goes along for the ride." Once in the water, though, the salt dissolves. That leaves the blobs of oil on their own. And without the salt to weigh them down, they float back up.

TOP TIP!
If the effect slows down or stops, just add a little more salt.

WHAT HAPPENS IF...?
Supermarkets stock many different types of cooking oil. You could try this experiment several times, using a different oil each time—perhaps sunflower oil, rapeseed oil, or olive oil. Based on the results, can you judge which of the oils has the highest density?

REAL-LIFE SCIENCE

The lava lamps from the 1960s and 1970s had blobs of colored wax at the bottom of clear tubes that were filled with liquid. A bright light beneath the tube would warm the wax, making it less dense. Blobs of this less-dense wax would rise up through the liquid, then cool down, become denser and sink to the bottom of the tube again.

The Citrus Candle

"It's a little dark in this corner... could you light an orange to help me out?" OK, so you'll probably never hear that request in real life, but the amazing thing is that you could use an orange if you ran out of household candles. How? Well, that's down to science, naturally.

1
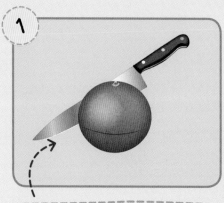

Ask an adult to hold an orange with the stalk at the top, and cut all the way around the middle, taking care to cut no deeper than the skin.

2
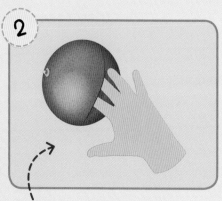

Hold one half of the orange and work your thumb or fingers carefully along the cut, sliding just under the layer of the skin.

3
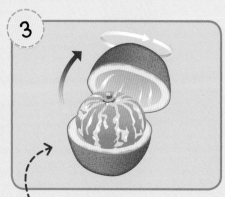

Twist the two halves slightly as you carefully pull them apart.

Put the half that doesn't contain the orange flesh to one side. Carefully remove the flesh from the other half, making sure you don't pull out the stalk.

4
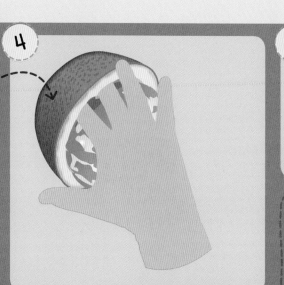

5
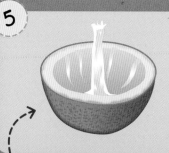

You should now have an empty orange half, with the stalk sticking up in the middle.

6

Slowly pour olive oil down on to the stalk, so that it almost fills the emptied orange half.

7

Ask the adult to light the stalk with a match and turn off the lights in the room, to get the full effect of your citrus candle.

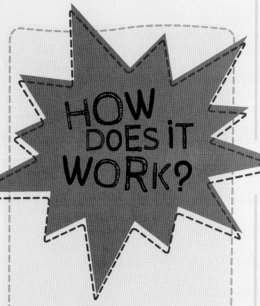

HOW DOES IT WORK?

WHAT HAPPENS IF...?

Try making this citrus candle following exactly the same instructions, except that you fill the orange half by pouring carefully from the side. In other words, you keep the olive oil away from the stalk. Before having your adult light the match, predict whether the candle will burn more quickly, more slowly or not at all. Then test the result.

REAL-LIFE SCIENCE

The olive oil in this candle (and the melted wax in a household candle) moves upward toward the flame. This movement of a liquid is called capillary action, and plants get water from their roots in the same way. The tiniest blood vessels in your body are called capillaries, and they move blood back and forth with the help of capillary action, too.

Any type of candle acts by burning a fuel, which warms until it becomes a gas, or vapor. A gas is a state of matter, usually reached when a material is warmed up from being in a different state—such as a solid or liquid. The olive oil was the fuel in this candle, going from liquid to gas as the candle burned. The wax in a normal candle goes from solid to gas, although sometimes you see a bit that's melted. It has become liquid first, but then flowed away from the heat so that it can't become a gas.

The Burning Rope Trick

Magicians sometimes do funny tricks with rope, causing it to rise up or even to seemingly dance. You can try a little scientific magic with some rope—OK, thread—that should produce some gasps. How about burning it, but finding it's still there?

1

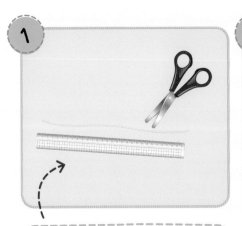

Cut a length of thread about 18—20 inches long.

2

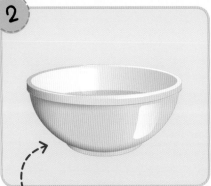

Half-fill the bowl with warm water from the faucet.

3

Add 4 teaspoons of salt and stir.

4

Put the thread in the bowl and let it soak for a minute, then let it dry.

5

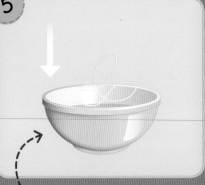

Repeat step 4 three more times.

6

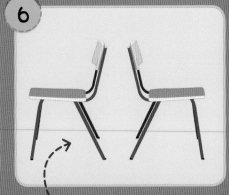

Set the chairs up back-to-back, with about a 6-inch gap between the tops of the chairs.

7

Place the ruler so that it spans the gap between the chairs.

8

Tie one end of the thread to the curtain ring and the other around the middle of the ruler; the curtain ring will now hang between the chairs.

9

Ask an adult to light the thread just above the ring.

10

The flame will move up the thread, leaving a thin column of ash behind—but the ring will still be held up!

An adult needs to be present and light the matches in this experiment.

TOP TIP!

Be very patient when soaking and drying the thread.

Continued

HOW DOES IT WORK?

The key to this experiment is—you guessed it—the salt. The salt dissolves in the water, which means a solution forms. It forms more easily if the water is warm. The thread soaks up some of that salt solution; when you dry the thread, the water evaporates and leaves the salt behind. If the solution is very salt-heavy, the salt can form crystals as the thread is dried. The magic? Well, that's because the salt crystals burn at a higher temperature than the cotton thread. The string is now a thin column of salt, the thread having been burned up!

WHAT HAPPENS IF...?

The trick is to make sure the string soaks up enough of the salt solution, and that the solution is salty enough. You can use the "scientific method" of careful repetition of the experiment to work out how much salt is needed. Start with a small amount, and if the ring falls, try a little more; keep going until it works.

REAL-LIFE SCIENCE

Maybe you have "sea salt" in your kitchen. It's basically salt water, but without the water. In some flat, coastal areas, each tide delivers a layer of water, which rests in shallow puddles on hard ground. As the tide recedes, and the Sun beats down, the water evaporates and the sea salt is raked up for collection.

Heavy Weather

Barometers measure air pressure, which helps predict the weather. They are some of the most sensitive scientific instruments. They can be very complex in their setup, but you can make your very own with just a glass and a straw!

- Drinking glass or glass bottle
- Balloon
- Scissors
- Plastic drinking straw
- String
- Modeling clay
- Paper and pencil
- Tape
- Table by a wall
- A friend would come in handy

1

Cut a piece of balloon in the shape of a circle—about 2 inches wider than the mouth of the glass or bottle.

2

Stretch that piece across the mouth, holding it tightly in place just below the rim.

3

Tie the string around the glass or bottle (or ask a friend to help you with this), keeping the rubber stretched tightly across the top.

4

Form a piece of modeling clay about the size of a large pea and roll it to get it soft.

5

Place this modeling clay on the center of the stretched balloon rubber.

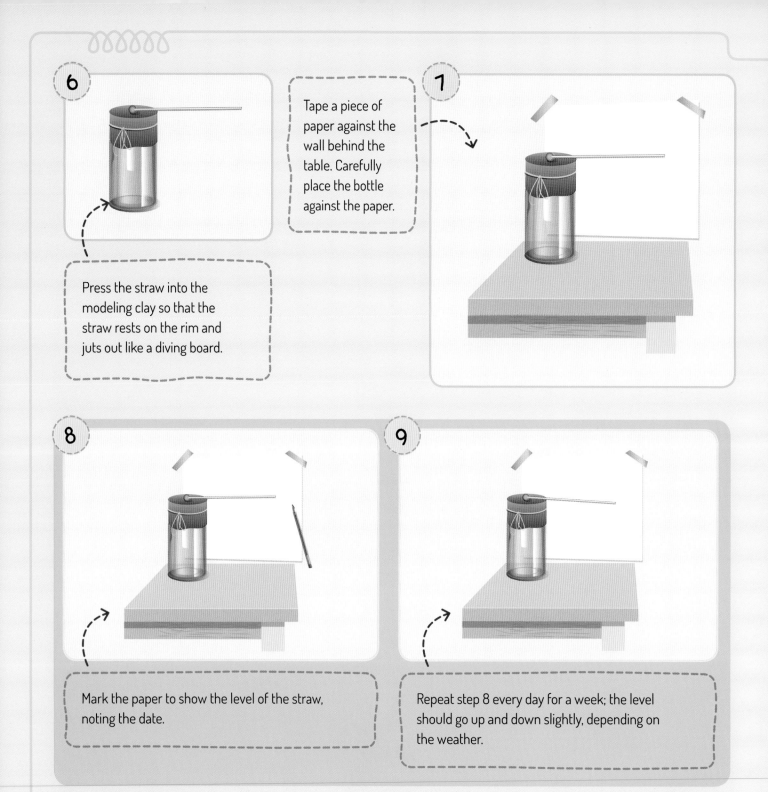

6

Press the straw into the modeling clay so that the straw rests on the rim and juts out like a diving board.

7

Tape a piece of paper against the wall behind the table. Carefully place the bottle against the paper.

8

Mark the paper to show the level of the straw, noting the date.

9

Repeat step 8 every day for a week; the level should go up and down slightly, depending on the weather.

TOP TIP!

Make sure to do this experiment away from direct sunlight and any other source of heat. That's because heat will affect the way the straw moves, while you want the results to show changes in air-pressure only.

HOW DOES IT WORK?

You've just done an experiment that deals with one of the main states of matter—gas. Air is a mixture of gases and, like any gas, it can change shape and volume. You've probably heard of compressed air. That's simply air that has been "pressed" into a smaller volume. Changing weather is usually a result of changing air pressure. Fine weather usually accompanies high pressure. This means that it presses down more on the rubber seal, squeezing the air inside. With the rubber moving down, the far end of the straw goes up—like a seesaw. Your markings should show rises and falls as the fair weather comes and goes.

WHAT HAPPENS IF...?

Try to predict what would happen if you used a different material to cover the mouth of the glass or bottle. Perhaps plastic wrap or cooking foil? What are the qualities of the balloon rubber that might make it behave differently? Test and observe.

REAL-LIFE SCIENCE

Monitoring air pressure is one of the most important features of weather forecasting. You'll hear forecasters predicting rain if there is a low-pressure front coming in, or reassuring people if high pressure is set to remain over a holiday weekend. Forecasters use highly sensitive barometers, which can pick up the slightest changes in air pressure.

The Pushy Candle

A candle flame can do all sorts of things: light a room, give some warmth or even make a room feel cozier. But can you imagine putting it to work and getting it to push or shove things around? You can, though, if you know how to harness the right forces.

1

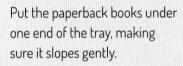

Put the paperback books under one end of the tray, making sure it slopes gently.

2

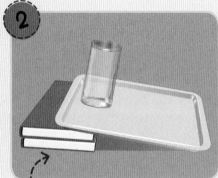

Wet the rim of the glass all around and set it upside-down at the higher end of the tray.

3

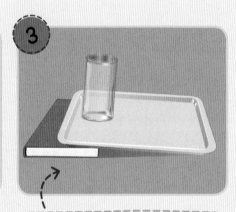

The glass should stay in position; if it begins to slide, remove one of the books.

4

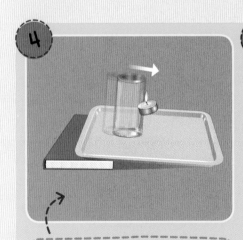

Ask an adult to light the candle and hold it very close to—but not quite touching—the side of the glass.

5

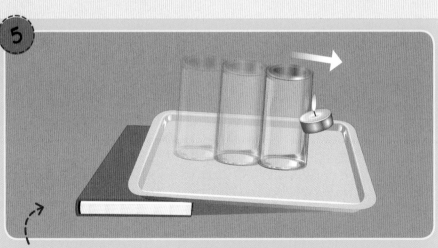

The glass will begin to glide mysteriously and smoothly down the slope of the tray. Make sure the adult follows the course of the glass, keeping the candle close to it.

HOW DOES iT WORK?

The floating glass traveled along on a cushion of air, which you helped to produce. The heat from the candle warmed the air inside the glass. The gases in the glass expanded as the temperature increased, pushing the glass up from the surface of the tray. This meant that the rim of the glass was no longer touching the tray itself—instead the rim was resting on the water. The surface tension of the water kept the rim in contact with the tray, so the heated air didn't escape from the glass. Without the friction of the glass touching the tray, the glass moved easily across the surface of the tray.

TOP TiP!

The candle can be held on any side of the glass, as long as it's close enough to warm the air inside.

WHAT HAPPENS IF...?

Remember that you need a gentle slope to make this experiment work at its best. If the tray is too level, the glass won't move, even though it will have the expanded air inside it. But if the tray slopes too much, the glass could tip over because it has become unstable.

REAL-LIFE SCIENCE

It's not just upturned glasses that can travel easily on a cushion of air. Large vehicles, called hovercrafts, work on a similar principle. Powerful fans send air down below the hovercraft, allowing it to lift up off the water. With less friction than a boat (because it doesn't touch the water), the hovercraft can complete sea crossings more quickly than standard ferries.

Getting Fizzy-cal

You don't need to be a lawyer or a judge to know that laws need to be obeyed. And laws don't just apply to people—everything in nature behaves according to laws that scientists have observed. Here's one you can test at a birthday party!

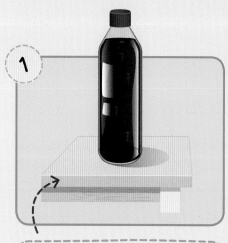

1 Keep the bottle steady and place it on a table or counter.

2 Slowly remove the lid.

3 Slide the mouth of the balloon over the mouth of the bottle.

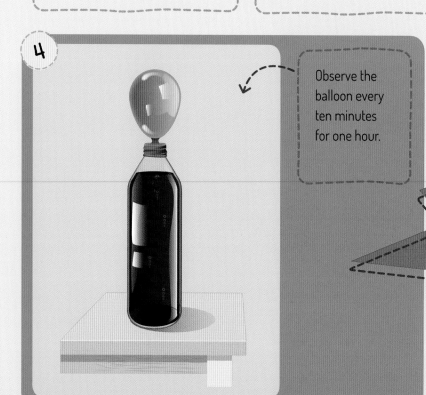

4 Observe the balloon every ten minutes for one hour.

You're on safe ground here, but just make sure you don't shake the bottle before opening it—it would ruin the experiment and make a mess.

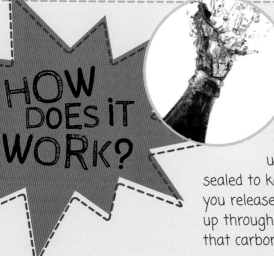

HOW DOES IT WORK?

Soda fizzes because of a gas—carbon dioxide—that's dissolved in the liquid. A chemical principle called Henry's Law says that the amount of gas that can be dissolved in a liquid increases in line with the amount of pressure being applied. Carbon dioxide is added to drinks under high pressure and then the bottle (or can) is sealed to keep the pressure high. When you opened the bottle, you released the pressure, so that the carbon dioxide bubbled up through the drink and emerged in its gas form. And it's that carbon dioxide that filled the balloon.

TOP TIP!

You can do this experiment inside or out, but just make sure conditions aren't too windy if you're outside.

WHAT HAPPENS IF...?

The Internet has thousands of "home movies" showing bottles of diet cola creating huge sprays after some mints have been dropped into them. That dramatic reaction is really a high-speed version of the release of carbon dioxide when you open a soda bottle. Seen up close, the candy has tiny bumps—the dissolved carbon dioxide latches on to these bumps and turns back into gas incredibly speedily.

REAL-LIFE SCIENCE

Dissolved gases can be dangerous. Deep-sea divers need to return to the water's surface slowly, because the high pressure of deep water causes some of the gases they breathe in (from their tanks) to become dissolved in their blood. Coming up too fast and releasing that pressure quickly could cause the gases to bubble up in the blood.

Water From the Sun

YOU WILL NEED

- Spade
- Polyethylene sheet (about 3 feet square)
- An old coffee mug
- 4 bricks (or 4 large stones)
- 2 friends

We'll put the "adult needed" warning right up-front in this experiment: you'll need an adult's permission to dig a hole in the lawn. Not just anywhere—you want this hole to catch the most sunlight. After all, you're collecting water. What?! Let science explain the magic.

1 Find a spot in the yard that gets a lot of sunlight, but doesn't have flowers already growing there.

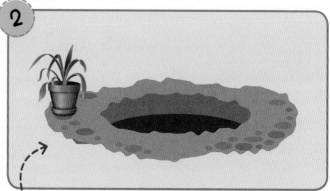

2 Ask an adult to dig a circular hole, about 1 ½ feet across and 1 foot deep; keep the soil you dug near the hole.

3 Set the mug at the bottom of the hole, in the middle.

4 Lay the polyethylene sheet across the hole, so that the hole is below the center of the sheet.

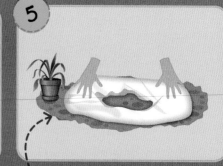

5 Ask each of your friends to press down on two corners of the sheet. Place soil, bit by bit, on the center of the sheet—directly above the mug.

6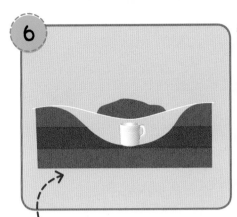

Stop adding soil when the polyethylene is almost, but not quite, touching the mug.

7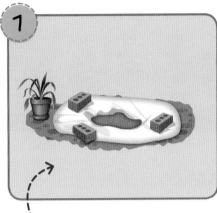

Place a brick on each corner of the sheet—your friends can stop pressing down.

8

Leave for three hours. Carefully remove the bricks and sheet—the mug will have begun to fill with water!

HOW DOES IT WORK?

You've just demonstrated condensation, a change of matter that occurs as a gas becomes a liquid. Water vapor (the gas form of water) becomes liquid water as it condenses. If it cools suddenly—as happens if the gas touches something colder—drops of water form. That's what happens when the warm air finds the cooler (inside) surface of the polyethylene. Drops of water form on that side. And because you weighed down middle of the sheet, the drops flow down and gather at the lowest point of the sheet before dripping into the mug.

TOP TIP!

It's best to wait for a sunny day to do this experiment, to make sure that there's a real clash of temperatures.

Continued ▶

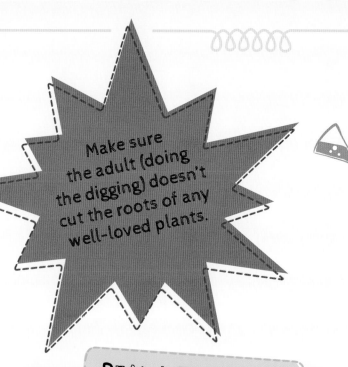

Make sure the adult (doing the digging) doesn't cut the roots of any well-loved plants.

TOP TIP!

When placing the bricks or stones on the sheet, make sure the sheet doesn't slip and touch the mug.

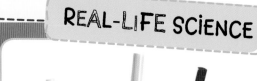

REAL-LIFE SCIENCE

In addition to being dependent on changes in temperature, condensation needs a surface where the liquid can form. You've probably seen it happen on a glass holding a chilled drink, or even with the "fog" on the inside of a car windshield. Tiny bits of dust are constantly floating around in the atmosphere. Water vapor condenses on these dusty flecks... to form rain!

WHAT HAPPENS IF...?

The hole in the ground is important in this experiment, and it's all down to the temperature of the air. Even a small hole like this one has cooler air than outside—think of it as a tiny cave. So you've found a way to cool the air on one side of the sheet. What would happen if the mug rested on the lawn, with the polyethylene above it?

Living Things

You can play detective (yes, even with fingerprints) as you explore how living things use science to survive and grow. What is more, you and your friends will become objects of some of the experiments!

Make a drum using peas and water (p. 112)!

The Damp Drumbeat

Some experiments boil down to one thing: having fun. Or maybe we should say "finding the whole thing funny." That might not sound very scientific, but it's the only way to describe how most people find this easy experiment about how plants get water.

1

Set the larger baking pan on a table or counter, and the smaller one upside-down on it. This placement will help with sound effects later.

2

Put a handful of the dried peas in the jar and place the jar in the center of the smaller baking pan.

3

Carefully fill the jar to the top with cold water.

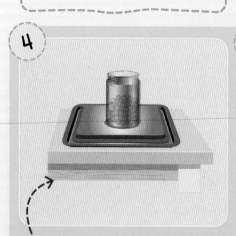

4

Wait for 15 minutes—listen and observe.

5

Swollen peas should fall from the jar on to the baking pan, landing with a "ping."

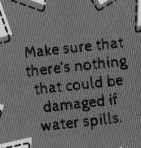

Make sure that there's nothing that could be damaged if water spills.

HOW DOES IT WORK?

This experiment is all about the way water moves through the cells of plants and animals—a process called osmosis. It's what happens when you put a dry sponge in water. The sponge draws in water until it's as wet as the water around it. That's what happened to the peas. As they absorbed water, they swelled up. That meant that they began to take up more space, gradually filling up the jar and falling out, one by one. Your double-pan arrangement made it easier to hear each pea falling out.

TOP TIP!

Most types of dried peas will work in this experiment, but the best results come from ordinary garden peas that have been sold dried.

REAL-LIFE SCIENCE

Osmosis is a form of passive transport. The other sort of transport ("active") needs energy to work. Just think of how your heart pumps blood through your body. Passive transport relies instead on the basic chemical process of osmosis. The tissue of plants and animals allows water to pass through in each direction, helping to supply nutrients and take away waste.

WHAT HAPPENS IF...?

Try doing the same experiment, but using fresh peas instead of dried. If they're not in season, drain some peas from a can and use those. How long will you have to wait until they start making that "ping" sound, one by one? Make a prediction and test it.

Testing For Prints

YOU WILL NEED

- Baby powder (or corn flour)
- Clear tape
- Black construction paper (letter size)
- Hand lotion
- Small paintbrush or make-up brush
- Magnifying glass (optional)

You hear the phrase "test the room for prints" every time you watch a detective at work on television. You know it means fingerprints, but just what are they? How do they get left? What do they look like? Solve those mysteries with this next experiment.

1

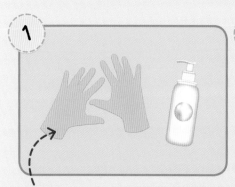

Rub a small amount of lotion on your hands, concentrating on your fingertips. Find a smooth surface area, such as a counter top or the edge of a sink.

2

Press two or three fingers down on that surface; this will leave fingerprints.

3

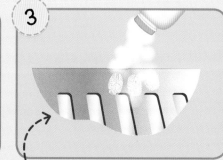

Sprinkle a little bit of powder on the surface where you have left the fingerprints; you should be able to see them.

4

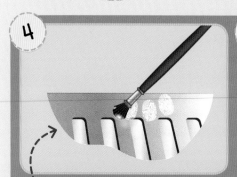

Lightly brush away the excess powder from the prints.

5

Carefully stretch a piece of tape over the prints and press down on the surface.

6

Lift the tape (which has the prints on it now) and carefully press it on to the black paper. You can use a magnifying glass to look at the prints closely.

HOW DOES IT WORK?

Your skin produces oils to keep it from drying out. Some of this oil is left behind when you touch anything, but it's hard to trace on many surfaces such as rough wood or cotton. Fingers do leave a clear trace behind, though, on smooth surfaces (we have enhanced this effect by using lotion in step 1). The raised, curled ridges on your fingertips leave a pattern: fingerprints. Normally you wouldn't notice them, but the sprinkled powder ("dusting") causes them to show up. And the careful transfer of those marks (you used clear tape) means that the prints can be studied far from "the scene of the crime."

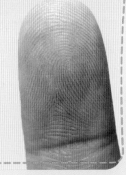

TOP TIP!

Press firmly, but not too firmly, when you leave the prints.

WHAT HAPPENS IF...?

Of course, knowing how to leave—and test for—prints is only half the fun. You could mark a section of paper and have your friends each press a finger into some ink. Then they could press their finger on to the paper. With each person's prints recorded, you could really begin to play detective by trying to identify whose prints are on the counter!

REAL-LIFE SCIENCE

Fingerprints are especially important because no two people have the same pattern of ridges on the surface of their fingertips. That means that everyone's fingerprints are unique. Detectives can match fingerprint evidence with suspect' prints to see whether there's a link to a crime scene.

Feel the Burn

YOU WILL NEED

- Clothepin
- Watch or timer (e.g. from a cell phone)

You've probably heard people talking about how important it is to "feel the burn" when they're working out in the gym. But just what is burning? Is there any to find out without needing to take a shower afterwards? Or burning up? Yes—with this experiment!

Hold the clothespin at arm's length and prepare to time yourself.

Count how many times you can squeeze this clothespin in a minute; the point is to score as high as possible.

Continue counting until the minute is up, or the 'burn' gets a little too extreme.

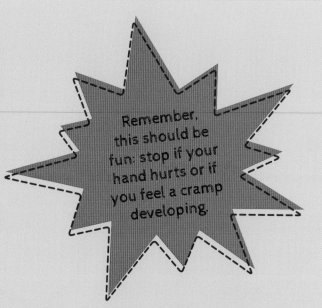

Remember, this should be fun: stop if your hand hurts or if you feel a cramp developing.

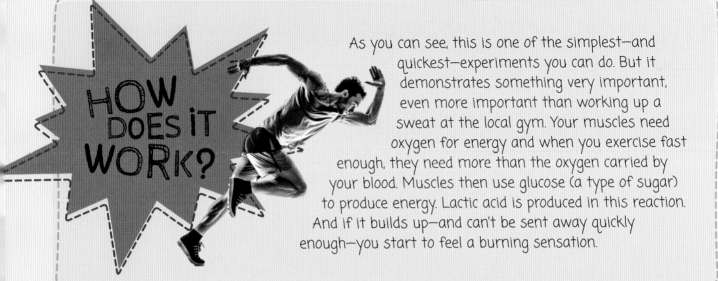

HOW DOES IT WORK?

As you can see, this is one of the simplest—and quickest—experiments you can do. But it demonstrates something very important, even more important than working up a sweat at the local gym. Your muscles need oxygen for energy and when you exercise fast enough, they need more than the oxygen carried by your blood. Muscles then use glucose (a type of sugar) to produce energy. Lactic acid is produced in this reaction. And if it builds up—and can't be sent away quickly enough—you start to feel a burning sensation.

TOP TIP!

Don't worry if you stop before the minute is up—you'll probably start feeling the burn by then anyway.

REAL-LIFE SCIENCE

Energy can be measured in calories. People can lose weight by reducing the amount of calories in their diet... or by burning them through exercise. "Feeling the burn" is a sign that lots of calories are being burned off—but people can get the same result without the burn. They just need gentler exercise over a longer period.

WHAT HAPPENS IF...?

What if you do it slowly? Speed is part of the key to it all. Think back to those images of people in the gym "feeling the burn." It's always quick-moving exercises that get that reaction: slow, gentle movements (as in yoga) call for stamina over the long term, and not quick, high-powered energy drains.

Hold the Line

YOU WILL NEED

- 1 bean seed
- Small flowerpot
- Potting soil or compost
- Cotton thread (cut to about a 15 inch length)
- Plastic straw
- Drawing pin
- Sheet of cardboard (ledger size)
- 2 heavy books
- Water
- Pen

Planting a seed and watching it grow is one of the joys of life, but sometimes we... lack... the... patience... to notice that growth. It might seem hard to tell whether the plant is growing healthily if it's only growing a part of an inch each day. Is there a clearer way of monitoring that growth? Yes—try it yourself!

1

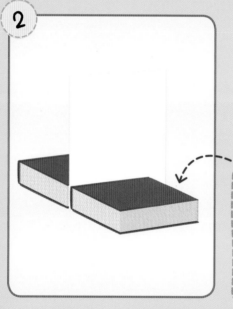

Soak the bean seed in water overnight, then plant it in the pot filled with soil or compost.

2

Line the two books up next to the flowerpot and stand the cardboard between them, so that it's upright; press the books together to keep it firm.

3

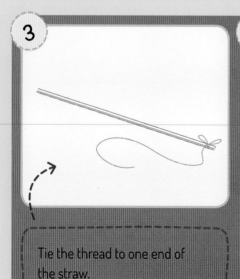

Tie the thread to one end of the straw.

4

Stick the pin through the middle of the straw and pin it to the cardboard. The pin should be about 6 inches higher than the top of the flowerpot and 6 inches in from the cardboard edge nearest to the flowerpot.

5

Check that the straw can spin around the pin. Then leave it in a vertical position with the thread at the bottom.

6

Follow the instructions about watering the soil. When the first shoot appears, tie the loose end of the thread to it.

7

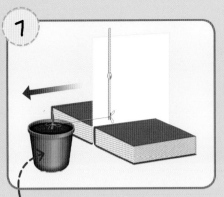

Gently move the pot away from the books until the thread is taut, with the straw still in its vertical position.

8

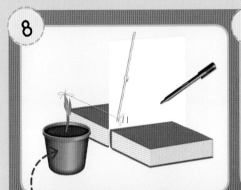

Pencil in a mark next to the bottom of the straw and date it.

9

As the plant grows, the thread will pull the straw around like the hands of a clock; mark each day's position.

It's hard to go wrong with planting a seed, but make sure that you don't drop soil or the flowerpot.

TOP TIP!

If you can manage it, try piercing the end of the straw with the pin point, and looping the thread through the small hole—there's less chance of the thread slipping off that way.

Continued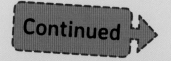

HOW DOES IT WORK?

This experiment depends more than anything else on the bean growing. You've given it the ideal conditions to prepare for growth. Soaking the seed triggers a mechanism that tells the seed there's enough moisture to germinate (or begin to grow). The soil or compost, coupled with regular watering and sunlight, help to provide ideal growing conditions. Once the seedling has popped out, it begins to tug the thread upward. This movement is translated into a curved motion (of the straw). Scientists and engineers describe a force that causes a rotation as "torque." It's the same force that turns a car's axle, but you've used it to power the straw.

WHAT HAPPENS IF...?

Like many of the best scientific experiments, you can change some elements (known as variables) that combine to make it work. One of the most obvious, of course, is to compare the growth of different seeds. You could even predict whether a different seed would grow faster, or higher, than the bean.

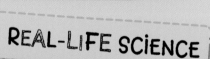

REAL-LIFE SCIENCE

Growing healthy, tall plants (sometimes as quickly as possible) has a scientific name: agriculture. Scientists (and farmers) are constantly looking for plant types, known as strains, that grow best in difficult conditions. They can even make money by selling the seeds of the best-performing plants.

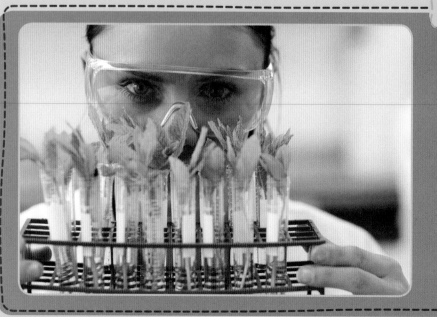

Stop That Landslide!

Landslides occur when the ground on a slope is unstable. They're dramatic and often destructive. Some of the same conditions lead to the less sensational, but equally destructive effects of soil erosion. Could plants come to the rescue?

YOU WILL NEED

- 2 plastic seed trays, each about 9 x 6 x 2 inches
- 2 identical high-sided baking pans, larger than the seed trays
- Soil from your garden or potting soil
- Radish seeds
- Food scale
- Ruler
- Watering can
- Water
- Paper and pencil
- Scissors
- 2 ice cube trays

1

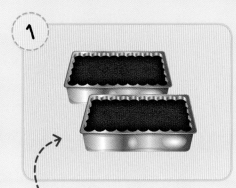

Fill each seed tray almost to the top with soil; leave ½ inch at the top.

2

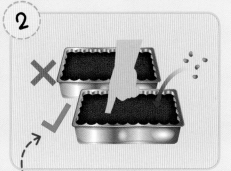

Plant radish seeds in one of the trays, following the instructions, but putting them closer together than suggested.

3

Weigh one of the baking pans using the food scale and record the weight.

4

Put each seed tray on a baking pan and place them side by side in a sunny spot—inside or out (as long as the weather is warm enough).

5

Water each tray carefully once a day for the next seven days.

6

After seven days, the plants should be about 3 inches tall; you can check with the ruler.

7

Make two vertical cuts halfway down a short side of each seed tray; the cuts should be near the corners.

8

Fold down each flap that you've just made.

9

Set each seed tray so that the "flap side" is inside the baking pan but the other end juts out beyond it.

10

Slide an ice cube tray under each jutting-out bit of seed tray. They should both be tilting into their baking pans.

11

Count to five as you water each of the seed trays, making sure that the water from the watering can covers all of the tray; don't worry if some water hits either side.

12

Remove the seed trays and you should now have two baking pans containing soil and water; drain off as much of the water as you can.

13

Weigh each baking pan, recording the results.

Subtract the earlier recorded weight (step 3) from each of the results in step 13; the result shows how much the washed-off soil weighs.

HOW DOES IT WORK?

This experiment turns your baking pans into miniature "hillsides," and you have measured how much soil runs off with rain. That's a huge cause of soil erosion. Plant roots act as anchors, causing the soil to clump together and resist being washed away. Maybe you've seen how soil sticks to the roots of plants—even weeds—that you pull up. You ignored the instructions about spacing the plants because this experiment is about those roots, and you want the crowded seeds to produce a tangle of roots. You can thin the plants out—for better growth—after the experiment.

TOP TIP!

Remember that you're trying to reproduce the effects of rain, which falls evenly over the ground, so try to water from high enough to produce that effect on the trays.

WHAT HAPPENS IF...?

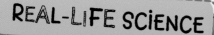

You can become really scientific by testing how effective different plants are. This would call for more time, as you'll be starting over, as well as the cost of a few more baking pans. But you could do several tests at once, trying different types of seeds.

REAL-LIFE SCIENCE

Many parts of the world have lost valuable farming land because of soil erosion. Being able to anchor the soil with plants is an excellent way of protecting against heavy seasonal rains, which cause so much damage. "Plant anchors" can even work in sand: many coastal areas are planted with types of beach grass to protect the dunes.

Making Breakfast

Live! From your kitchen! We bring you some breakfast yogurt! In fact, YOU'LL be bringing the yogurt once you've done this experiment. And before long, you'll see why the word "live" is so important. Bacteria never tasted so good.

YOU WILL NEED

- Live yogurt (you may need to find it in the health food section)
- Whole milk
- 2 small mixing bowls
- Small glass thermometer
- Microwave oven
- Tablespoon
- Dish towel

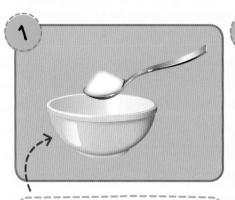

1 Scoop out 4 tablespoons of yogurt into a bowl.

2 Warm the bowl in a microwave for about 2 minutes, until it's 107–111 °F.

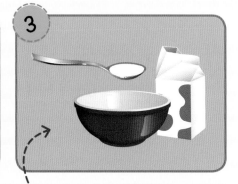

3 Add a tablespoon of yogurt to the second bowl. Now stir 4 tablespoons of warm milk into that second bowl.

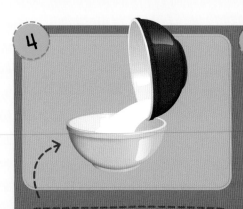

4 Add that mixture (yogurt and milk) into the first bowl. Stir well to spread it evenly.

5 Cover the bowl with a dish towel and put it back in the microwave (which should be closed—to keep in heat—but not turned on).

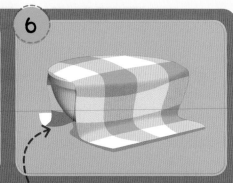

6 Leave for 10–12 hours and uncover. You should have thick, delicious yogurt!

HOW DOES IT WORK?

This is all about bacteria. These tiny organisms eat the lactose (a type of sugar) in the milk to gain energy and to reproduce. Lactic acid gets produced as a result, and these acid molecules react with the protein in the milk. Those protein molecules, in turn, get reshaped so that they stick together. The "sticking together" quality is what we recognize as yogurt. "Live" yogurt means that it contains the bacteria that will be needed to start the process. And as you saw, you only need a little yogurt from one batch to turn a much larger amount of milk into more yogurt.

TOP TIP!

Remember—this experiment only works with live yogurt, preferably bought on the same day.

WHAT HAPPENS IF...?

Like many science experiments, you can learn a lot if it doesn't work. If you're a little cruel, you can have a contest with a friend to see who can make the best yogurt. Don't tell them that you need to start with live yogurt, so let them use a different type. As long as you use the live variety (and remember the instructions) you'll win every time!

REAL-LIFE SCIENCE

No one knows for sure who first discovered yogurt, but many people believe that it was in the Asian region of Mesopotamia (modern Iraq) more than 5,000 years ago. It might even have been an accident—some goat's milk might have turned to yogurt in the warm conditions.

How tall is that tree?

YOU WILL NEED

- 2 yardsticks (with meter measurements)
- Tree in an open space (e.g. in a park)

Imagine being able to measure the height of a tree without having to climb it. You could guess, and maybe get pretty close to the right measurement. Or you could use engineering, which ties science to practical jobs. And just like a real engineer, you'll use the metric system to make things easier to work out.

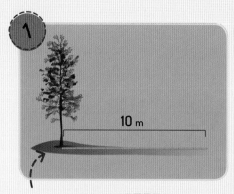

1 The first step is to find a tall tree—but one that you can see clearly from top to bottom. Start at the base of the tree and measure 10 meters out from it.

2 Hold one measuring stick vertically, with the zero pointing down.

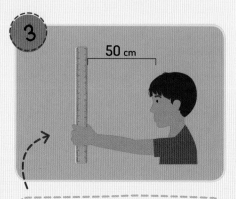

3 With your other hand, hold the other measuring stick out in front of you, so it's about 50 cm from your eyes.

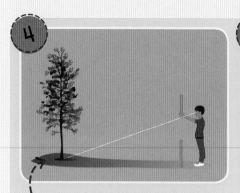

4 Move the stick up or down until the base (zero end) lines up with the base of the tree.

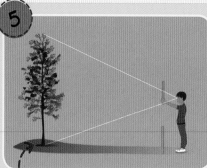

5 Hold the measuring stick steady and note where the top of the tree crosses the measuring stick.

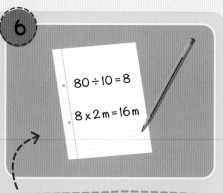

6 Each 10 cm mark will equal 2 m of height; for example, if the top of the tree matched 80 cm on the stick, it would make the tree 16 m tall (eight 10-cm marks multiplied by two).

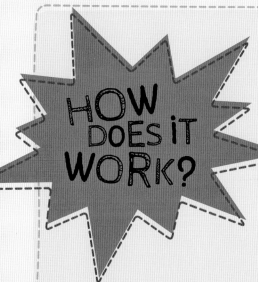

HOW DOES IT WORK?

You've created an engineering tool called a hypsometer, a device to calculate height or altitude. Engineering is where science and mathematics meet—this experiment uses triangulation to work out the height. As you might expect, triangulation involves triangles. You had two triangles in this experiment, one being a mini-version of the other. The big one's sides were the connection between your eye and the top of the tree, your eye and the bottom of the tree, and the tree trunk. The small one was the same, just with the third side being the stick. Knowing the length of the stick meant that you could work out the tree's height.

TOP TIP!

A tree in a park or someone's yard is ideal, because your view of it isn't blocked by other trees or vegetation.

REAL-LIFE SCIENCE

Not all hypsometers use triangulation to work out height or altitude. Some measure the temperature at which water boils and calculate altitude. The higher the altitude (for example, on a mountain), the lower the temperature at which water boils. Precise measurements of height or altitude can help with forest regeneration, tree surgery, and plant studies.

WHAT HAPPENS IF...?

What if you don't have room to walk 10 meters out from a tree? You could do the same experiment walking out five meters. The result would be even easier to calculate: each 10 cm mark on the stick would mean 1 meter of tree height.

Glossary

acceleration The increase of velocity.

air pressure The constant pressing of air on everything it touches.

atom The smallest possible particle of a chemical element.

bacteria Single cell microorganisms, some of which are used to make foods, such as yogurt and cheese.

center of mass The point that has the mass of an object evenly distributed around it; also called the center of gravity or balancing point.

circuit The closed path that an electrical current follows.

climate The weather pattern of an area.

combustion The process of burning.

conduct To transmit heat or electricity.

current (electrical) The flow of electricity along a wire or through a substance that conducts electricity.

density The amount of mass something has in relation to its volume (or space that it takes up).

disperse To scatter.

electromagnetism Magnetism that is created by an electrical current.

electron A negatively charged particle that forms part of an atom.

energy The power or ability to do work such as moving. Energy can be transferred from one object to another, but it cannot be destroyed.

equilibrium Balance between two or more objects or forces.

evaporate To turn from liquid into vapor (gas).

force The strength of a particular energy at work.

frequency How often something occurs.

friction The force that causes a moving object to slow down.

gravity The force that causes all objects to be attracted to each other.

hydraulic Powered by putting pressure on a fluid.

ignite To catch fire or begin to burn.

inertia The way matter continues in its existing state, unless changed by an external force.

insulation Material that prevents or slows the transfer of energy from one object to another.

kinetic energy The energy of movement.

magnetism A force, related to electrical currents, that creates an attraction between certain materials.

mass A measure of how much matter something contains.

meteor A piece of rock or metal that moves through space.

molecule The smallest unit of a substance, such as water, that has all the properties of that substance.

momentum The amount of movement an object has, measured by multiplying its mass with its velocity.

nutrient Any substance that the body needs for energy or growth.

osmosis The process by which a less concentrated (more watery) solution passes through tissue to mix with a more concentrated solution, in order to create an equilibrium.

particle A very small piece or amount of something.

prism A clear, solid object that refracts light as it passes through, so that it is broken up into the colors of the rainbow.

radiation Waves of energy sent out by sources of light or heat.

refract To cause waves (of light, heat, or sound) to bend as they pass through a different material.

sound A vibration that passes through air, water, or other materials and which the ear converts to recognizable impulses.

stamina The ability to endure hard effort over a long period of time.

static electricity Electricity that is held or discharged (sent off) by an object.

surface tension A force that binds molecules on the outer layer of a liquid together.

velocity The speed of something in a particular direction.